For my new best friend:

....

PARISIAN CHIC

A Style Guide by Ines de la Fressange

Translated from the French by
Louise Rogers Lalaurie

Design
Noémie Levain

Copyediting
Lindsay Porter

Typesetting
Thomas Gravemaker and Claude-Olivier Four

Proofreading
Kiki in Paris

Production
Murielle Meyer

Color Separation
Couleurs d'image, Boulogne-Billancourt

Printer
Worzalla, Wisconsin, United States

All photographs by Ines de la Fressange
and Sophie Gachet, except the following:
Benoît Peverelli p. 25, 27, 29, 31, 33, 35, 37, 41, 45, 49
Spa Nuxe 32 Montorgueil p. 189
Tibo p. 77
Deidi von Schaewen p. 192
Fabrice Vallon for Très Confidentiel p. 190
All rights reserved p. 76, 81, 84, 89, 90, 97, 102, 103,
147 bottom, 188, 222 top, 199–201, 204, 226
Thierry Chomel p. 222 bottom

11 12 13 7 6 5

ISBN: 978-2-08-020073-0
Dépôt légal: 04/2011

PARISIAN CHIC

A Style Guide by
Ines de la Fressange

with Sophie Gachet

Illustrations by Ines de la Fressange
Photographs of Nine d'Urso by Benoît Peverelli

Flammarion

Contents

PART 1

Dress Like a Parisian

1. Parisian DNA

You don't need to be born in Paris to have Parisian style—I'm the perfect example, born down south in Saint-Tropez! Parisian style is an attitude, a state of mind. Between rocker and *ho-hum* bourgeois, a Parisian is always first, never second. A Parisian steps lightly around the fashion traps of the day. Her secret? She breathes the *air du temps* and puts it to good use, her way, and always with the same aim: fashion should be fun. The Parisian follows a few golden rules, but she likes to transgress, too. It's part of the style. Here's my six-point guide to the Parisian gene code. *C'est facile!*

Outfits are out

Coordination is a crime—mix it up!
Knowing how to mix styles and labels
is essential. A clever mix of chic and cheap
hits the jackpot when it comes to dressing
à la Parisienne. Teaming a vintage It bag
with a basic cashmere sweater takes more
flair than slavishly copying the latest runway
styles. The Parisian is a free spirit—she
does not buy a matching blouse and skirt
from the same store. The rule is simple:
chic means never having to buy a complete
outfit. To be reinforced constantly.

Bye-bye bling

Vive la Rive Gauche!
Left Bank Parisian style travels
well, and stands out in a crowd.
The Left Bank Parisian stalks the streets of
Saint-Germain-des-Près, steering clear of
anything bling. Never look rich—glitter
and logos are *not* her thing. A true Parisian
is not looking to snag a billionaire husband.
She is uninterested in spending for its own
sake and sporting the labels to show for it.
She seeks chic, and demands quality.
Her definition of luxury? A brand that
guarantees good taste, rather than an
all-too obvious price tag.

Explore! J'adore...

The Parisian loves discovering new labels, especially if they're creative and affordably priced. She will rave about a great find in the humble supermarket (yes, *really!* Parisians adore the Monoprix chain), but never fights to be first with the latest high-priced It bag, especially not if it's waiting-list only (so vulgar…). Her wardrobe is a clever mix of cheap and affordable buys, holiday purchases, and a handful of luxury pieces. Impossible to tell if her jeans or denim jacket are from Gap, Notify, H&M, or Hermès! She won't blow her salary on the latest "must-have" she can't afford it, for one thing, plus she has faith in her own talent as a fashion stylist: why spend so much on something she could have designed herself? The Parisian knows she will never go out of style. She sweeps fashion aside (but she always sports a telling detail gleaned from the latest trends). It's part of her charm.

If it feels good, wear it

You'll never hear a Parisian complain that her skirt is too short, her dress too tight, or her heels too high. Fashionistas and style gurus all come to the same conclusion: "The secret of great style is to feel good in what you wear." The Parisian knows her shape, what suits her, and what matches her lifestyle. If you don't feel comfortable in a plunging sweater, skin-tight jeans, and killer heels, go home and change!

INES

Worship no idols

The Parisian never worships fashion idols.

She is a fashion icon in her own right (but she
still secretly admires Jane Birkin and Charlotte
Gainsbourg, and their faultless offbeat style: grey
cashmere sweater + jeans + Converses or vintage
boots = the ultimate aspirational look). And she
adores her super-stylish best friend (every Parisian has
one) who sports a look all her own, never outdated,
all while sailing serenely into a *certain âge*.
Her personal fashion idol may not be famous.
The more obscure the better, in fact. Like the best
designers, she takes inspiration from the street.

Beware of good taste

Who knew that black and navy were made for each other?

No one — until Yves Saint Laurent gave us
permission to boldly go where no one had gone
before…. Today, the unlikely duo is a must for
every elegant soirée. Know how to take liberties with
fashion's sacred dictates. Some rules are meant to
be broken, including the ones in this guide, *bien sûr!*
You love orange dresses with yellow shoes? Go for it!
Everyone will want to copy you some day. Fashion
is constantly evolving, and that's what makes it so
interesting. The day will come when Parisians decree
that mini-shorts with leopard-skin bomber jackets and
studded ballet flats are the best things since sliced
bread. Be prepared….

Shopping coach

→ **Who can honestly say they've never been tempted by a dress covered in sequins or a flouncy petticoat skirt?** The Sirens of the fashion world are hard to resist, but resist you must. Every Parisian learns the rules of the art of shopping: if you keep a clear head when faced with such an abundance of choice, you'll keep a wardrobe free of things you'll never wear.

Don't be a fashion victim

Think first

✳ Always ask yourself: "If I buy this, will I want to wear it tonight?" If the answer is "*non*," or "I'll wear it around the house," or "Maybe one day, to a party, you never know," it's time to leave the store, and fast.

Listen to the sales staff

✳ OK, there are always those with an eye on their commission, but most sales staff will know their collections inside out, and can quickly find the right item for you. *It's what they do….* On the flipside, avoid anyone who declares your every choice is "*very* popular this season!" The Parisian hates buying something that everyone else is wearing. She pays more attention to what suits her than what's on the runways, which she professes to ignore (see next point).

assimilate trends

✱ Following fashion is something the Parisian hates, but she still needs to know what's in. The trick is never to follow current trends slavishly. Even if leopard-skin prints are top of the list this season, she will not step out looking like she's escaped from the Paris zoo. A faux leopard- or zebra-skin clutch is enough to proclaim her credentials as a woman of style, not a follower of the herd.

Don't buy "works of art"

✱ We've all bought an item of clothing saying, "It's so lovely and bright, what a beautiful piece!" We love it as an object in its own right, for its bright colors, its witty details. We love it for what it is, not what it can do for our style, our silhouette. Always think about how the piece will integrate into your wardrobe. Don't assume that a piece beautifully presented in the store, with perfect lighting, will inevitably be a good buy. In this way, you will never fall for that orange coat when you have auburn hair, or that flounced silver miniskirt when your thighs really aren't up to it. Recognizing fashion's limits is an art in itself!

Split your budget into two

✱ Use half for quality basics, and half for impulse buys that will brighten your wardrobe (a belt, a bag, costume jewelry). Even on an average budget, there are plenty of ways to achieve a great look—you'll find you need less than you think. A few really good sweaters, jackets, and coats will be far better: quality not quantity. Know how to eliminate non-essentials; saying to yourself "I'll keep this to wear when I'm painting the house," never works! Learn how to give things away; there are all too many people in need, and plenty of organizations to help them. One thing's for sure: a well-organized closet with a few choice pieces is the best way to start the day.

Mix it up

→ **Don't go for the head-to-toe!**
The Parisian's war cry says it all:
the pursuit of offbeat chic
(with added irony) is her favorite
sport. Two or three zany details
can transform a look, with madly
successful results. But mixing
it up can be risky. We are all just
steps from a fashion faux pas,
but the true Parisian will find
a way to snatch a *triomphe de style*
from the jaws of disaster. She knows
that too many rules, too closely
followed, are never a good idea. Resist
the head-to-toe look of the ladies-who-
lunch at all costs! Here are my Top Ten
ideas for an offbeat look *à la Parisienne*
(in reverse order of risk).

LESS
is
MORE

10 _Jeans with gem-encrusted sandals_
(not sneakers)

 9 _a pencil skirt_ with ballet flats
(not with heels)

 8 _a sequined sweater_ with men's trousers
(not with a skirt)

 7 _a diamond necklace
with a denim shirt,_ during the day
(and not with a black dress at night)

 6 _Loafers with shorts...
and even with socks_
(not with long slacks and no socks)

 5 _An evening dress_ with ultra-plain, open-toed
sandals (not with the gem-encrusted evening variety)

 4 _a pearl necklace_ with a rock' n' roll T-shirt
(not with a simple shift dress)

 3 _a chiffon print dress_ with battered
biker boots
(not with brand-new ballet flats)

 2 _a tux jacket_ with sneakers
(not _femme fatale_ stilettos)

1 _An evening dress_ with a straw handbag
(not with a gold clutch)

Effortless style

→ **"Effortless style" often takes, as it says, relatively little effort.** All you really need is loads of self-confidence … and a smile. (You can carry off anything with a smile!) Of course, a few tips can help you achieve your own effortless (or almost effortless) style. Here are sixteen of mine:

✳ *Wear* a little wool sweater with your ball gown. Stoles are so kitsch, really—avoid them at all costs: even Hollywood stars have given up on stoles for the red carpet.
The same goes for little bolero jackets. A sequined dress with a cashmere sweater, now that's pure Paris!

✳ Shop at H&M, in the *menswear* department.

✳ *Mix* couture and street culture. Wear beautifully-tailored, perfectly-cut pants with a super-soft, ultra-fine cotton T-shirt (younger girls can try a print). Why choose between the up-scale vs. casual look? You can do both, in style!

✳ A *parka* over a little chiffon dress.

✳ *Wear two* scarves, one on top of the other. This works equally well with two T-shirts, two blazers, even two belts. Turn the spotlight onto the most basic elements of your wardrobe.

✳ One *maxi-impact* accessory with an ultra-simple silhouette. The Parisian worships Jackie in her Onassis period: white pants, a black T-shirt, open-toed sandals, and oversized sunglasses. Chic, effective, and oh-so-easy to copy, right now!

THE UNIVERSAL GOLDEN STYLE RULE

Wear full pants and skirts with tight-fitting tops, and tight trousers and skirts with loose-fitting tops.

✳ *Team* your old, worn-out denim jacket with a silk blouse. As with a T-shirt and tailored pants, the combination gives your look instant depth and "edge." Keep everything else ultra-plain and simple. The idea is to look as if the luxury item — the silk blouse — has been slipped on almost by accident. Appearing to try too hard is very uncool: everyone knows the Parisian buys truckloads of fashion magazines to keep abreast of current trends, but she never lets it show! (She may even buy this guide and tell her friends it's for a gift).

✳ When you're bored with your clothes, dye them *navy blue* for a new lease on life. (Unless they're already navy blue, *bien sûr!*)

✳ Have your traveling friends bring back kurti shirts from *India*, in a host of colors. Wear them under a cardigan, with pearls: preppy meets ethnic chic!

✳ Wear black velvet riding jackets a couple of sizes *too small.* Ditto traditional blue French work jackets.

✳ Hunt for *vintage* men's scarves and wear them with everything.

✳ Anything from a *surplus* store worn with vintage costume jewelry is good.

✳ Wear your teenage son's *shirt* with a push-up bra underneath. (And don't try to hide it!)

✳ Cinch everything with a big, well-worn man's *belt*. Tie the excess length in a loose knot.

✳ Wear knee-high cashmere *socks* in all colors (khaki, raspberry, turquoise).

✳ *Roll* the sleeves of your cotton shirt back loosely over your sweater — the ultimate casual chic statement.

2. Not-So-Basics

Brilliant basics are

the key to a great look! Parisian style is simple
(well, almost). Make sure your wardrobe includes
the Magnificent Seven: a man's blazer, a trench
coat, a navy sweater, a tank top, a little black
dress, jeans, and a leather jacket. After that,
it's all a matter of composition. What effect
are you aiming for? How to transform your basics?
What to avoid? Here is a user's guide for that
"made in Paris" look.

The blazer

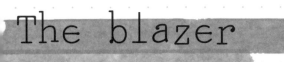

The essential look

* The masculine/feminine. And definitely *not* the masculine/masculine. You have to know how to give it that feminine touch.

The transforming touch

* Belt it!

* Push back or roll up the sleeves — the ultimate "easy chic" statement. Even better when the lining's a different color.

* For daytime, wear it with pants in a contrasting color (jeans are always good).

* For evening, match the jacket and pants (black on black, a perennial favorite).

* Wear it with a white shirt casually unbuttoned at the top for a subtly sexy look. A lace, silk, or satin camisole adds a further touch of chic.

Fashion faux pas

→ A miniskirt with a masculine blazer — an ultra-feminine skirt kills the jacket's impact.

→ An oversized jacket with linebacker shoulder pads. No, you can't! Keep it fitted.

Celeb style

Navy blazer + white chiffon shirt + white jeans: a clean, crisp look that suits everyone!

Hall of fame

The Yves Saint Laurent tuxedo jacket. Wear it as the man himself suggested, with nothing but a bra underneath. Obviously the YSL version isn't within every woman's reach, but its fabulous success means it has been widely copied by affordable chain-store labels. *Merci!*

The trench

The intended look

You've been wearing it forever,
like a second skin.

The transforming touch

*   Roll or push up the sleeves
and scrunch the collar to make
it less rigid.

*   Never, ever buckle the belt
properly like a good little girl. Tie it
in front or behind with the buckle
hanging loose. Unobtrusive fashion
statements like this ("Life's too short,"
or "The buckle's broken but I love this
coat so much I found a solution…")
are very, very Parisian.

Celeb style

With jeans, dinner-suit pants, over
a little black dress—is there any
occasion when a trench coat will
not do? It goes over everything
and with everything!

Fashion faux pas

→ The military look. Never
over-emphasize the (wartime)
"trench" aspect of your trench coat….

→ With a long skirt.
No one wants to look like a statue
or a chess-piece.

→ With a twin-set, rope of
pearls, straight skirt, and hair band.
Avoid this particular fashion statement
(which says very clearly "No fun …!").
Unless you are sixteen years old, with
an extra helping of irony.

→ In polyester.

Hall of fame

The Burberry, *bien sûr!* Plenty
of other versions look the same
from a distance, without the
legendary lining, but it's still
a great look.

The navy sweater

The essential look

Clean-cut but not too straight-laced. Understated, but more sophisticated than a plain black sweater. (Admit it: sometimes black sweaters are just too easy!)

The transforming touch

✱ White jeans. Two items just made for each other.

✱ Black pants, in honor of Yves Saint Laurent's brilliant way with chic color combinations.

✱ With flat shoes for an "easy cool" look.

✱ With heels and a bunch of bangles for evening (think "clink" not "bling").

Celeb style

White jeans + V-neck navy sweater + high-heeled sandals + leather jacket.

Which fabric?

Cashmere, of course. Too expensive? Not true! Parisians snap up the cashmere collections at chain-store sales and rave about their finds at Monoprix stores throughout France. Remember that cashmere lasts far longer than other wools or fabrics, wash after wash!

Fashion faux pas

→ Navy blue is risk free, unless you wear it with yellow (in which case you are sailing dangerously close to the brand colors of a certain Swedish furniture store).

Hall of fame

Any navy sweater is timeless! Éric Bompard (www.ericbompard.com) is often cited as the official supplier of virtually every Parisian. But New Yorkers (Gap) and Tokyo-ites (Uniqlo) have their favorites, too!

The tank

The essential look

A classy supporting act. The tank is there to accompany your look.

The transforming touch

✳ Shorts, jeans, even a skirt (especially a print skirt).

✳ A good-quality necklace.

✳ Under a tuxedo jacket or blazer.

What color?

Keep it simple: black, gray, white, navy, khaki. Avoid supposedly fashionable shades like pine green or red, which may be great for making your children easy to spot on the beach—but that's about it.

Fashion faux pas

⟶ Skin-tone shades. Who wants to look naked?

⟶ Patterned tanks. Too obvious.

Celeb style

White tank + beige pants + blazer + sandals with heels.

Hall of fame

The tank chez Petit Bateau, of course! France's favorite label for sleepwear and other basics is a must-have for any true Parisian. Take the children's size (age 16) for a super-stylish, tight, stretched look. Or try the Rolls-Royce of tanks, from Abercrombie & Fitch: long, straight, and beautifully cut, it falls right back into place after every wash.

The little black dress

All about the little black dress

* The little black dress is not simply an item of clothing, it's a concept. It's abstract, it's universal — which means there's one that's perfect for everybody. In fact, "the" little black dress is a misnomer: everyone wears hers differently. Think of a modestly dressed Edith Piaf, with her hands pressed flat against her stomach. Or a magnificent Anna Magnani in tears, in a neorealist Italian film. We all have our own particular idol.

* Today, the Parisian has several little black dresses, just as she has several pairs of jeans: each is a variation on a theme. The little black dress is an open secret: we all know it will save us whatever the situation, and whatever the continent, the season, the time of day, the man…. Why?

* Because the little black dress is the epitome of sexy and elegance. Which is *not* a contradiction in terms.

The essential look

Simplicity, simplicity, simplicity … with a healthy dose of elegance.

Celeb style

With huge black sunglasses (1980s-style, from Persol) and black ballerina pumps. Add long black gloves for winter, and you're all set for breakfast on the sidewalk terrace outside Tati Or (Paris's cheap neighborhood jeweler), *à la* Holly Golightly (a.k.a. Audrey Hepburn) in *Breakfast at Tiffany's*.

Hall of fame

Suddenly, there it is, all alone on the clothes rack. The perfect little black dress just made for you. There's one in every boutique, waiting to become the key item in one woman's wardrobe.

The perfect jeans

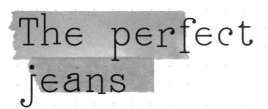

The essential look

Once upon a time, we had just one pair of jeans. Now, it's fun to have several. Sky-blue, navy, black, white — to match the season, or your mood!

What shape?

✳ The battles rage, with fashionistas currently wavering from skinnies to "boyfriend" and back. One thing is certain: straight-leg jeans are without a doubt the most timeless cut of all. The Parisian's favorite shape is easily worn with anything. Personally, I love low-waisted jeans, but that's a question of body-shape.

What color?

✳ Sky-blue, washed, and dark: three shades of denim to see you through every season. A black pair is compulsory, with white for a brighter touch. After that, it's up to you, to mix with your favorite colors. And don't forget navy-blue jeans, too, a good alternative to untreated denim.

How not to wear denim

✳ Jeans are never too risky; they're a bit like salt — they go with everything!

When to wear white?

✳ Who said white jeans were for summer only? I strongly recommend white jeans for winter, worn with a navy sweater and ballet flats. They're also great at night, with a silver sequined jacket — perfect for the most elegant soirée!

Celeb style

Used denim + tuxedo jacket + patent brogues (wing tips) + printed neck scarf.

Hall of fame

When it comes to jeans, the most iconic model of all is the one that suits you best.

The leather jacket

The essential look

Guaranteed to save any overly-conventional look.

The transforming touch

✱ With a chiffon dress, to avoid the "garden party" look.

✱ In winter, under a coat, adding a touch of rock'n'roll to an overly elegant look. Feel free to let your sweater show underneath.

✱ With a rope of pearls. A winning offbeat look.

✱ The older (or more distressed) the better. When you buy it, put it under your mattress for several nights before wearing it, or walk all over it. Alternatively, buy a vintage model—you'll sleep better.

Fashion faux pas

⟶ Never with biker boots. We are not Marlon Brando.

Celeb style

Tan leather jacket + white jeans + silk top + heels.

Hall of fame

The best leather jacket is close fitting, with slim sleeves and two patch pockets. You might find yours where you least expect it. I found mine on sale at Paris designer Corinne Sarrut. Tan is always tasteful.

3.Spotlight on Accessories

The Parisian builds her look around fabulous basics, so accessories are *the* key to her personal style. It doesn't matter if you're tall or small, slender or curvy—accessories are the easiest things to adapt to your shape. And if you invest in quality accessories, you can go for more affordable clothes—nobody will notice. Accessories are all-important!

Parade of shoes

→ Women often express their fantasies in their footwear: shoes are the symbol of what we want to be. Which explains why some women buy shoes they will never wear. We love shoes like we love bags—we have plenty already, but we can't resist the call of the new. And because we know how a simple pair of shoes can transform our whole look.

all about heels

Many women think they look better in heels, but this is quite wrong. Just ask any man. No man would ever say "I'd love you more if you were four inches taller!" And remember, many women have no idea how to walk in high heels. Nothing looks worse than a girl tottering about on unmanageable heels! So she wants to look sexy? The key to sex appeal is a feline walk, not a precarious wobble. I know girls who have ended up on crutches because they wanted to walk tall without mastering the rudiments of striding with confidence in eight-inch heels. Practice first, at home!

Every Parisian's shoe collection contains...

Ballet flats

From E. Porselli in Milan (or at APC, www.apc.fr and SAP, 106, rue de Longchamp, Paris 16e). When you're tall like me, and tired of being asked, "Are you sure you need heels?" every time you step out in a pair of pumps, you find yourself wearing ballet flats 24/7. Happily, there are *ballerines* for every occasion. Gold for day and black suede for evening is always elegant. With pants or dresses—everything goes! If you had to choose just one pair of shoes, these would be the ones.

Open-toed sandals

Impossible to get through the summer without them! France's favorite classics are found only in Saint-Tropez, at Rondini (or online at www.rondini.fr). K. Jacques, also made in Saint-Trop', are an alternative choice, (www.kjacques. fr or in Paris at 16, rue Pavée, 4e. Tel: +33 [0]1 40 27 03 57). But Parisians will always admit that the best ones are found down south in Saint-Tropez. Remember—Parisians are incredible brand snobs.

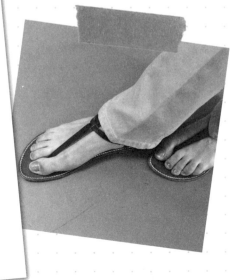

Black heels

One fine pair of black heels will last a lifetime. It's worth investing in the best you can afford. Shapes change, and toes are sometimes round, sometimes pointy, but choose an ultra-classic design (neither too pointy nor too round) and you'll clock up hundreds of miles without the need for a pit stop to search for a more up-to-date pair.

Penny loafers

Absolutely essential, but wear them with care, to avoid looking like a preppy caricature. Never with a pleated skirt, of course but then, who wears a pleated skirt these days? Team with chunky socks and jeans just short of your ankle. And remember to slip the eponymous penny inside the front slot, for good luck. Simple!

Riding boots

With a skirt, a dress, or even with shorts and tights, for the under-35s. Knee-high boots are the winter equivalent of ballet flats. In black or tan, the best ones really look like genuine riding boots. Some Parisians are even known to buy theirs in specialist equestrian boutiques.

It's in the bag

→ The bag is central to every Parisian's personal style. It can make life easier (with special pockets for your phone and lipstick, a spring clip for your keys, an integrated flashlight) or make life hell (the big bucket bag into which everything is thrown together, and in which even a cat would have a hard time finding her kittens). Choosing the right model is all-important. The Parisian chooses her bags on impulse, and not because she has been told what to carry around this season. She is uninterested in the latest It bag, but very keen to find *the* iconic bag for her.

memo

Better a genuine straw bag than a fake luxury label! Counterfeit is *counterfashion!*

✳

It's almost impossible to commit a fashion faux pas when choosing a bag (except for backpacks and banana-shaped fanny packs or bum bags). From animal-skin prints to flaming red, anything goes!

✳

By all means match the color of your bag and shoes if you're under 30. After that, prepare to age ten years....

Five essential models

The big tote bag

A faithful friend for every day. You can slip your clutch inside — handy if you are going out after work and can't go home first. Take out your clutch, and leave your tote bag at the office!

The clutch

The essential evening accessory — or for daytime use if it's big enough and soft enough. Perfect for raising the tone if you've under-dressed, especially if it's a "couture" model with embroidery, beads, or luxury fabrics.

The satchel

For a casual touch —
and a guaranteed antidote
to It-bag-itis!
A satchel is for life…

The ladies' handbag

Solidly-structured, in neutral
shades (black, natural, tan).
A timeless classic that has seen
the ups and downs of popularity.
The Parisian will tell you hers
belonged to her grandmother.
But everyone knows she had it
made to order chez Hermès.

A straw bag

Your summer friend,
à la Bardot in Saint-Trop'.
Parisiennes carry theirs around
town, for a touch of offbeat chic.
A guaranteed style statement.

Diamonds are a girl's best friend

24/7 brilliance

Who still thinks diamonds should only come out at night? I have a *rivière* necklace that belonged to my grandmother. I wear it during the day over a T-shirt, and if anyone asks where I got it, I tell them it's paste! (I sometimes wear paste, too, but no one can tell the difference nowadays!)

memo

Don't pile on your engagement ring, your eternity ring, and a bracelet loaded with charms from the birth of each of your four children: your most beautiful item of jewelry is your wedding ring.

Avoid ostentatious, sophisticated luxury pieces. Instead, opt for something minimalist, like a single stone simply set, or a tourmaline ring from Marie-Hélène de Taillac (www. mariehelenedetaillac.com).

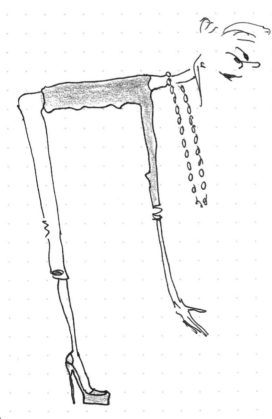

Five pieces guaranteed to make a statement

Antique earrings

Never out of style (they already date from centuries past).
By day, or at night, they adapt to any and every style.
Hoop earrings are good, too.

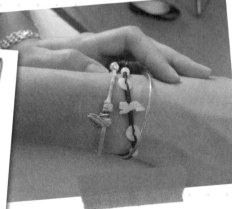

A lucky charm bracelet

Especially when it's been brought back from India and you can tell your friends, "I'd give you the address but it was a gift from a friend, she brought it back from India…"

NEVER. EVER.

A chunky necklace with big earrings—you do not want to look like a Christmas tree!
If you want to mix it up, choose very delicate, very unmatching pieces.

A man's watch

A big, man's watch with a
cashmere sweater, jeans, and
Converse sneakers is very sensual.
And with a tuxedo jacket
or a little black dress, it's sexy.

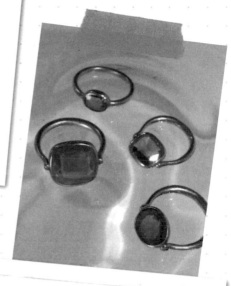

Colored gem rings

Gold rings topped by precious or semi-
precious stones are truly timeless. Some
people claim the different stones have life-
enhancing properties: chalcedony is known
for its soothing powers, for example; citrine
is energy-giving; peridots protect from
harmful, negative influences and add a
cheerful note. Wearing jewelry to make life
even better—j'adore!

A cuff bracelet

A striking cuff will always make
a statement and stand out.
An armful of fine bangles is
another good investment.

4. Fashion S.O.S.

What to Wear, When

An improvised dinner with friends?
A wedding? A country weekend?
With just a few hours to spare, the Parisian
throws open her wardrobe. Need a style
upgrade in five minutes flat? Follow her
dress code for every occasion.

Dinner in town

What's up?

✳ You've been invited to eat out with friends in a fashionable restaurant. How do you look the part with no apparent effort?

Dress code

→ Bank on your basics—strictly no flouncy dresses. Keep it ultra-simple if you're not sure about the restaurant's dress code (fashionable restaurants can be anything from ultra-hip to ultra-chic). The make-or-break item? Your shoes. Try something original (a new color, killer heels, gemstones). If they're really off target, you can always hide them under the table!

A black-tie event

What's up?

✱ Obviously, some people receive more invitations to formal events than others, but a black-tie wedding is fairly certain to show up at some point on every social calendar.

Dress code

➝ Avoid buying this season's color if you don't have a host of other opportunities to wear this outfit again soon. We are constantly praising the virtues of the little black dress, so how about the long black dress, too? For a bright, witty touch, tie a colored ribbon at the waist (Parisians buy theirs at Mokuba, 18, rue Montmartre, 1er. Tel. + 33 (0)1 40 13 81 41). Heels are recommended but you can lay low, too—no one will object!

A dinner date

What's up?

✱ Whether it's a blind date or your first romantic evening, you're on a mission to seduce.

Dress code

➝ The Parisian detests anything too obvious. Showing her hand (and much more) from the outset with a plunging neckline and a micro-mini is not her thing. In winter, she may even opt for a turtleneck sweater. A man's plain white shirt with black pants (or pedal pushers for a lighter touch) and unobtrusive shoes will allow your potential mate to concentrate on the conversation. Lingerie? A push-up bra certainly helps, but keep it hidden for now!

A weekend in the country

What's up?

** The Parisian is often invited to the country for the weekend. How not to look like a hick in the sticks?

Dress code

⟶ Remove all outward signs of fashion. Leave your It bag at home and take a straw bag, a cotton tote, or a satchel instead. Put away your ballet flats and get out your Converse sneakers. Remove all items of jewelry except your man's watch. And bring out the basics: tank, T-shirt, and khaki pants. The only "themed" item permitted is a fisherman's sweater or navy and white striped *marinière*. Especially if you're not far from the sea.

A cocktail party

What's up?

** Every Parisienne is confronted from time to time with a cocktail reception — a private art gallery viewing, a literary award, the opening of a new boutique…

Dress code

⟶ Time to get out your tuxedo jacket (over black pants, white jeans, used denim) and add a high-profile, unmissable accessory (a fluorescent clutch, huge earrings, a giant cuff bracelet). The aim? To blend with any arty atmosphere. Your little black dress will also do the job. The right length? To the knee, or just below. Under-40s can opt for the mini — always attractive.

Pack Your Bags!

Traveling is a serious business—every Parisian likes to look good at the airport. She may not be snapped on arrival like the celebs touching down in Los Angeles with their pillows tucked under their arms, but the Parisian in transit keeps up appearances, always. Here's her checklist for flying in style:

- For long-haul flights, the Parisian slips into ultra-soft low-waisted velour sweat pants (check them out at Zara www.zara.com). Never a skirt, never a dress!

- A big, warm sweater is essential. Underneath, pile on the layers, starting with a tank, plus a long-sleeved T-shirt, ready to peel off as required at your destination.

- Moisturizer, lip balm, and eye drops. Hydration is everything

- Socks to slip on once you've taken off your shoes.

- Tennis shoes (Converse for me, of course). Don't even think about traveling in heels or boots. If you take them off to sleep, you'll never get them back on!

- A large tote bag to accommodate your books, magazines, and laptop.

- The Parisian loves to look as if she's traveling light: she'll always take two small, wheeled suitcases in place of one huge (back-breaking, heavy) one. And she is genuinely skilled in the art of not taking her entire wardrobe on holiday (all very well for stars heading to Cannes, but ridiculous when all you want to do is relax on the beach). As for the color of her suitcase (yes, nothing is left to chance!), black is best. Avoid garish palm-tree prints and bright colors that are supposed to "make it easier to spot at the baggage claim."

5. Fashion Botox

An ill-advised print dress can age a woman ten years! Always go for rejuvenating looks, which are just as effective as an anti-wrinkle injection—and so much more fun. How to give your style a facelift? Follow these tips *à la Parisienne.*

Change your style

→ **Never allow yourself to get stuck in a style adopted at a particular age: it will age you instantly!** This is especially dangerous past 40, when it's tempting to carry on dressing just as you did when you turned 30. You've just reached the end of that fabulous decade when you feel comfortable with your looks, everything suits you, and life is full of possibilities and good things—an exciting career, love, children—when you feel young and mature at the same time, and you don't want it to stop. In any case you haven't got time to think about a makeover!

✳ At 40, surprisingly, women start asking themselves the still somewhat unnecessary question: "Can I still get away with this?" And what surprises them most is not the answer, but the need to ask the question in the first place. In reality, there's still time, but better to face the question now than never! Above all, do not cling blindly to everything that suited you when you were 30. You've changed, times have changed, and fashion has, too. By all means carry on expressing your personal style, but never let that translate into boredom, a lack of interest in new trends, the absence of desire, clinging to habit and routine,

fear of change or making a mistake— NON! Accept that you will get some things wrong. Everyone makes mistakes when they're out shopping— take it as an (encouraging) sign that you still dream of reinventing yourself! For me, a loss of interest in dressing well and using make-up is a form of depression. Far from making radical changes, the Parisian knows how to *evolve* her style as she gets older.

Golden rule #1

Never follow convention.

*

Never be bland.

*

Never neglect yourself.

Golden rule #2

Always choose the right accessory to transform your look.

EXAMPLE

I often dress in navy or black with a white shirt, but sometimes on a whim I'll surprise everyone and go for a fuchsia pink blouse. Result: no one tries to work out how old you are.

Fashion faux pas
AT
50 +

Ethnic print tunics and dresses in African batik prints. Past a certain age, these look like costumes.

Preppy clichés (pearls or bead necklaces + earrings). Obviously.

Furs. Instant Cruella. The "wrinkled trophy wife" look can be very aging.

Big clip-on earrings. If you don't have pierced ears, choose a necklace instead.

Neon colors. Too readily associated with teen fashion.

Mini-skirts and micro-shorts. No Parisian would ever dress mutton as lamb.

Stay interested

✳ A great way to stay young at heart. Look out for new designers, try a new pants shape, get yourself some platform shoes. Be bold—even if it results in the occasional faux pas!

Sell your crocodile handbag on e-Bay

Never follow fashion blindly

✳ A beginner's mistake. Be aware of current trends and embrace their subtler forms: the color gray, wide-leg pants, peacoats…. Forget all about tartan, ripped jeans, studded thigh boots.

Always mix chic and cheap

✳ A pile-up of luxury labels can be fatal after 45.

Don't dress like a teenager

✳ No mini-skirts, humorous print T-shirts, etc. Trying to look young is the quickest way to look old.

Be bold

✳ Wear a bomber jacket in place of a blazer at night; ballet flats instead of heels with a chiffon dress. Pin your brooch to your hip, not your lapel. Or try military medals and badges in place of a brooch.

Avoid clichés

Change your jewelry regularly

✳ ...even a Scoubidou (i.e., boondoggle, lanyard) bracelet makes a difference!

Don't feel obliged to buy "fun" clothes

✳ A good-quality round-necked sweater is a must in any 50+ wardrobe: mix it with jeans and a rope necklace for a chic look that's never dull.

Loafers and ballet flats suit everybody

✳ As do tennis shoes (Converse are a religion for the Parisian). All are perfect for an appealing, fun look (even a political statement) at 50+.

Get dressed listening to "Dead Flowers" by the Rolling Stones.

Aging isn't just about what you wear

✳ Declaring that Twitter is stupid, you don't know how to use an MP3 player, and the iPad leaves you cold, spells "instant Oldie."... Beware!

6. Fashion Faux Pas!

Fashion changes with

the seasons. Gaucho pants will be shunned one year and worn in every color the next. The same goes for overalls, Norwegian sweaters, and thigh boots. Identifying fashion faux pas can be a tricky business in such conditions. But some looks and trends will *always* fail to flatter. Read on for the Parisian's most-scorned style blunders.

Lingerie

✳ Bras with transparent plastic straps.
No one ever gets used to them. A stylish, visible bra is far sexier, and if you really want to wear a strapless dress or top, how about a strapless bra, too?

✳ Thongs with ultra-low hipster jeans.
One of fashion's great mysteries.

✳ Visible thigh highs.
Unless you're on stage at the Crazy Horse!

✳ No matter how big or small your bust, *not wearing a bra is always a mistake.*

Jewelry

✳ never wear a necklace and earrings at the same time—too much! The same goes for rings on every finger. As for accumulating bracelet(s) + ring(s) + watch + earrings + necklace: *Non, non, non, non, non!* Even at Christmas….

✳ It should come as no surprise that *scarf rings are prohibited.*

✳ Body piercings.
"No future" is the wrong kind of fashion statement….

Swimwear

✳ Too sexy. bikinis. in lurex and sequins. Think Ursula Andress or Halle Berry in their Bond Girl briefs. Much more attractive.

✳ A swimsuit with too much lacing or complicated cuts. You'll see why when you take it off after a day in the sun.

✳ Bikini briefs too small to cover your bottom. The Parisian keeps a bikini line *à la Brazilienne*, but not the bikini to match.

Accessories

✱ White fringed boots.
There are more sophisticated ways to
achieve the Wild West look.

✱ Hair scrunchies.
Too girly.

**✱ Fanny packs or bum
bags.** Even if some designers are
trying to promote their comeback,
these are too practical to be attractive.
Just say *non*, whatever the season.
And especially if you're a tourist!

✱ Plastic flip-flops.
And pool sandals. Guaranteed
to shatter the chic-est of looks.

**✱ Sandals with white
socks.** Unless you're an actress
in a New York art-house film. In Paris,
the combination is practically illegal.

**✱ Matching tights,
shoes, and bag.**
No, you can't.

✱ Backpacks, once
you've left college.

**✱ Back-to-front
baseball caps.**
Ask yourself if a baseball cap—even
the right way around—is really a
good idea? Choose a sailor's cap
or a straw hat instead.

Clothes

✳ Too tight shirts that gape at the buttons across your (ample) chest. Choose an ample shirt instead, and never button it all the way up.

✳ Leggings. Seldom a good look on anyone.

✳ Leather suits. Even if leather is in this season. Even if Angelina dares to wear one. Even if you see them all over the magazines. By all means go for the leather jacket or pants, but never the two together. Too showbiz.

✳ Fishnet T-shirts. Difficult to see how these could possibly flatter anyone, apart from Madonna in *Desperately Seeking Susan*.

✳ Cropped T-shirts. Displaying your navel away from the beach is never chic. It's a matter of proportions.

✳ Leopard-skin dresses with plunging necklines. Too sexy is not sexy.

✳ nightgowns printed with favorite children's characters. I have never met a man who was seduced by a Hello Kitty nightie!

✳ Transparent pants. What's the point of wearing pants if they reveal all?

✳ Supposedly witty "message" T-shirts. "My boyfriend's out of town.", "Gold digger"…. Do I really have to explain why?

✳ Too many mixed materials. Satin + velvet + chiffon + tweed = textile overdose.

7. Parisian Fashion

Shop in Paris ...
or Online

Don't think the typical Parisian

spends all her time (and money) on ultra-luxurious Avenue Montaigne! Dior, Chanel, Louis Vuitton, Yves Saint Laurent, Hermès, Céline, and France's other luxury flagships are the bedrock of her fashion heritage, but she loves shopping in small, offbeat boutiques, too, tracking down hip labels and legendary hotspots. And now almost every Paris fashion temple has its own online boutique, delivering the City of Light to Parisians at heart, all over the world. Here are my favorites.

Sœur

The story

✱ Created by two sisters, this boutique was originally aimed at young girls. Thank heaven Domitille and Angélique Brion have created a delightful style that mothers find hard to resist, too.

The style

✱ Little girls get bigger every day…. My daughters always find up-to-the-minute shorts, T-shirts, and dresses at Sœur. But I love their style, too, in age 16—neat cotton shirts and sweaters, brilliant basics with a charming twist that keep perfectly from one season to the next. Stepping boldly into boutiques that don't appear to be for you—the essence of Parisian style!

The must-have

⟶ Neat mini-dresses to wear as tunics.

The perfect gift

⟶ The scarf, in a delicate floral print, perfect for anyone aged 7 to 77.

Paris: 88, rue Bonaparte, 6ᵉ
Tel. +33 (0)1 46 34 19 33
www.soeur-online.fr

IN A NUTSHELL

This is our little secret—don't pass this one on...

Vanessa Bruno

IN A NUTSHELL

i love that film you're showing in the boutique—what's the title? Oh, it's your latest ad campaign?

The style

✱ Romantic and feminine, with soft colors and fluid cuts. Vanessa Bruno is the queen of draped silhouettes. Each piece has a distinctive, creative touch, clearly designed by a woman who loves clothes that feel great.

The must-have

⟶ The sequin-trimmed tote is star, but each season a new design becomes a classic, and the heels are always über-comfortable, check out the lingerie and the cheaper, more casual Vanessa Bruno Athé label.

London: 1a Grafton Street
New York: 1273–1277 Third Avenue
Paddington, Australia: 29 Williams Street
West Hollywood : 8448 Melrose Avenue
Paris: 25, rue Saint-Sulpice, 6ᵉ
Tel. +33 (0)1 43 54 41 04
www.vanessabruno.fr

APC

IN A NUTSHELL

Of course my jeans are APC, but i like their candles and records, too.

The must-have

→ The standard straight-leg jeans, a truly great basic. With cuffs or without, a timeless VIP piece.

The style

✳ Ultra-basic but utterly timeless. V-neck sweaters, little dresses, bags, pants. Every Parisian has at least one APC piece in her wardrobe. And each new collection brings its crop of It clothes of the moment. They've recently begun stocking Porselli ballet flats, too.

New York: 131 Mercer Street
Paris: 38, rue Madame, 6ᵉ
Tel. +33 (0)1 42 22 12 77 and
112, rue Vieille-du-Temple, 3ᵉ
Tel. +33 (0)1 42 78 18 02
www.apc.fr

Isabel Marant

IN A NUTSHELL

Non-Parisians love Isabel's clothes, too: Eva Herzigova and Elle MacPherson bought the entire collection this season!

The must-have

→ A shirt, With new details each season, making every collection unique.

New York: 469 Broome Street
Paris: 1, rue Jacob, 6ᵉ
Tel. +33 (0)1 43 26 04 12
www.isabelmarant.tm.fr

The style

✴ Isabel's ethnic-chic styling is the key to her success. Embroidered tunics, fluid pants, flowing dresses—Marant clothes make you feel great. And the look is pure Parisian: beautifully-made clothes, no logo, not ridiculously over-priced, and as comfortable as your favorite jeans.

Maje, Sandro, and Ba&sh

IN A NUTSHELL

Your jacket, is it
a Balenciaga
or Maje/Sandro/Ba&sh?

The style

The Parisian's favorite sport is hunting down hip clothes at affordable prices. In addition to H&M and Zara, she never misses at least one of these three stores, overflowing with the latest looks. If epaulettes are in this season, you're sure to find them here, next to the sequined sweaters and denim shorts. These stores are everywhere in Paris, and spreading fast. Each offers its own variation on the basic theme— this season's top styles, now or never!

Maje: → Rock chic
London: 129 Sloane Street
Paris: 24, rue Saint-Sulpice, 6ᵉ
www.maje-paris.fr

Sandro: → Urban glam
London: 133 Sloane Street
Paris: 47, rue des Francs-Bourgeois, 4ᵉ
www.sandro-paris.com

Ba&sh: → Easy chic
Paris: 83, rue d'Assas, 6ᵉ
Tel. +33 (0)1 46 34 74 09
www.ba-sh.com

Éric Bompard

The style

✱ Cashmere, cashmere, and more cashmere. For winter or summer, this is the house specialty. The look isn't wildly creative—the sweaters are super-simple and perfectly cut, but they're just what you need for your wardrobe basics.

The must-have

➔ The V-necked sweater. Perfect.

IN A NUTSHELL

Every goat aspires to be a Bompard supplier.

Boston: 171 Newbury Street
London: 106–108 Kings Road
New York: 1095 Madison Avenue
Paris: 91, avenue des Champs-Élysées, 8e
www.ericbompard.com

Petit Bateau

The style

✱ A brand that can claim an unbroken lineage since 1893, this is *the* Paris childrenswear label. Cotton underwear from Petit Bateau is the Parisian's equivalent of Proust's *madeleine*—instant flashback to childhood. Today, the collection includes maternity wear and adult clothes, too (the designs for ages 18–20). Making your clients think they can dress like they did when they were 20—a clever move!

IN A NUTSHELL

My Petit Bateau undies are unsinkable.

The must-have

➔ The tank, part of Petit Bateau's brand heritage.

Paris: 116, avenue des Champs-Élysées, 8e
Tel. +33 (0)1 40 74 02 03
www.petit-bateau.fr

Liwan

IN A NUTSHELL

The incredibly nice owner has wonderful skin and uses their Alep soap herself. I bought seven bars!

The style

✳ A Lebanese store with a wonderfully warm welcome that will make you want to stay forever. Everything is in impeccable taste, from loose-fitting tunics to fabrics, decorative objects, and jewelry, giving instant character to any all-white piece. When I was pregnant, I wore their long linen shirts in summer—divine!

The must-have

⟶ Leather open-toed sandals in every color, and belts.

Paris: 8, rue Saint-Sulpice, 6ᵉ
Tel. +33 (0)1 43 26 07 40

PARIS EXCLUSIVE

Kerstin Adolphson

The style

✱ A Swedish boutique where everything comes from the frozen north. From clogs (the stars of the summer collection) to chunky knitted sweaters (taking the limelight in winter). Each year brings its crop of must-haves.

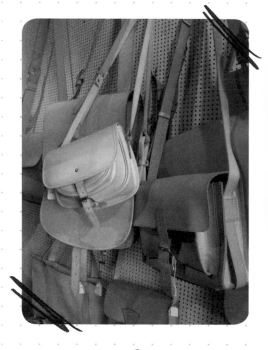

The must-have

⟶ The natural leather tote bag. When I carry one in the street I get stopped by girls wanting to know where it's from. These bags last forever, and acquire an attractive patina in the process.

IN A NUTSHELL

Ethnic chic from a cold climate.

Paris:
157, boulevard Saint-Germain, 6ᵉ
Tel. +33 (0)1 45 48 00 14
www.kerstin-adolphson.c.la

Swildens

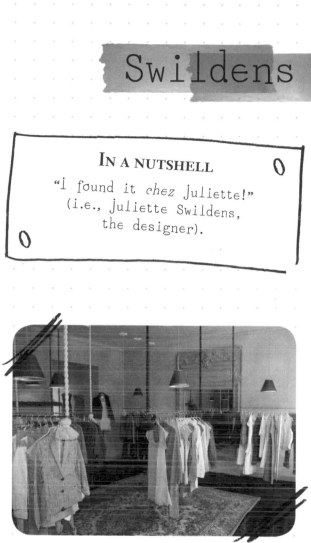

IN A NUTSHELL

"I found it *chez* Juliette!"
(i.e., Juliette Swildens,
the designer).

The style

✱ Romantic-rock, with a heavy dose of hip. Impossible to explain how they do it (magic?), but each season, Swildens comes up with the styles everyone wants. When fur vests were the It accessory, Swildens had them lined with stars, and everyone wanted one. The same goes for their floral prints or vintage scarves.

The must-have

⟶ I can't count the number of girls who've told me: "My leather jacket? From Swildens!"

Paris: 16, rue de Turenne, 4ᵉ
Tel. +33 (0)1 42 71 12 20
www.swildens.fr

Journal Standard de Luxe

The style

✳ A temple of what I can only describe as "luxury miserabilism." Their downbeat Japanese "Roots" collection includes oversized cashmere sweaters, pashmina tunics, boiled wool sweaters, vintage cropped shirts· I want them all. I adore their old-fashioned style, the fabulous fabrics and the "rustic-chic-gentlewoman" look you have when you wear them. A subtle selection, courtesy of a charming Japanese buyer. Nothing glitters—this is the temple of anti-bling—but everything has great appeal.

The must-have

⟶ Oversized sweaters in a variety of fabrics. Absolutely timeless.

Paris: Jardins du Palais Royal,
11–12, galerie de Montpensier, 1er
Tel. +33 (0)1 40 20 90 83
Japanese site, but ordering is a snap!:
www.journal-standard.jp

IN A NUTSHELL

It'll last a lifetime, no matter what. Your Visa card will wear out faster than that sweater you just bought.

Marie-Hélène de Taillac

The style

✱ Step inside the boutique, and you'll often hear someone insisting, "I'm not used to wearing precious stones!" Ever since her first collection launched in 1996, Marie-Hélène de Taillac has made women want to wear "real" jewelry every day, with pieces that don't look as if they've just been removed from the family safe for a night at the opera. Simple and incredibly refined, these precious gems have a touch of India about them—logically enough, because Marie-Hélène designs her ultra-luxury bohemian pieces in Jaipur, using colored stones guaranteed to put you in a good mood.

The must-have

⟶ Impossible to choose! I love the cabochon rings, and the *Frivole* ring with a pivoting stone.

IN A NUTSHELL

Did you know Marie-Hélène has a fashion boutique in Jaipur?

Paris: 8, rue de Tournon, 6ᵉ
Tel. +33 (0)1 44 27 07 07
Tokyo: 3–7–9 Kita Aoyama, Minato-Ku
US: Available at Barneys
For ordering close to *chez toi*:
www.mariehelenedetaillac.com

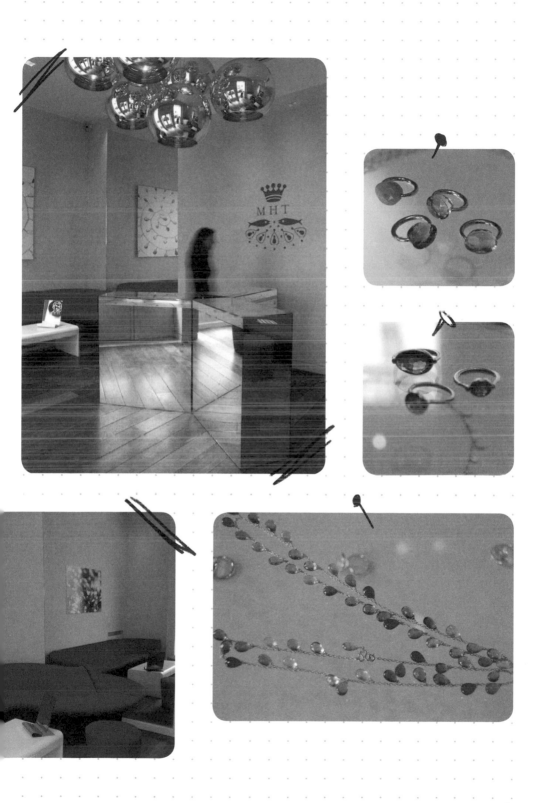

Adelline

The style

✴ Housed in a tiny shop, Adelline designs are minimalist, ultra-collectible treasures. Little stud earrings, long rope necklaces, or rings and bracelets set with cabochon stones—everything is *très* desirable, with a hint of Indian influence (Adelline takes inspiration from the Gem Palace in Jaipur). Each piece seems to tell a story.

The must-have

⟶ Too hard to choose…. The rings with colored stones are as covetable as sugar candy, while the gold bracelet ending in a snake's head is utterly hypnotic.

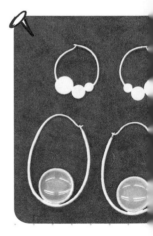

Paris: 54, rue Jacob, 6ᵉ
Tel. +33 (0)1 47 03 07 18

PARIS · EXCLUSIVE

IN A NUTSHELL

Send your husband there—even if he has terrible taste, he won't find anything ugly!

Pierre Barboza

IN A NUTSHELL

Old is
always new.

The style

✸ For lovers of romantic jewelry
from the 1830s, this mini boutique
looks as old as the treasures it
contains. It also sells "transformed"
pieces, with added stones for a new
lease of life.

The must-have

⟶ Everything is unique,
everything is a must!

Paris: 356, rue Saint-Honoré, 1er
Tel. +33 (0)1 42 60 67 08

PARIS · EXCLUSIVE

Dinh Van

IN A NUTSHELL

My mother's been wearing her Dinh Van bracelet for thirty years—these pieces are a sound investment!

The style

✱ The essence of delicacy and understatement, Dinh Van jewelry is for every day of your life. Parisians who hate bling love Dinh Van!

The must-have

➔ The super-simple bracelet or the rope bracelet with a gold ring.

Paris: 16, rue de la Paix, 2ᵉ
Tel. +33 (0)1 42 61 74 49
www.dinhvan.com

Emmanuelle Zysman

IN A NUTSHELL

Lucky me!
i managed to pick up a
"Lucky Link"
bracelet.
Definitely charming!

The must-have

⟶ The hammered silver gilt bracelet fastened with a cotton tag. Everyone will ask where you found your bracelet—so tell them!

Paris: 81, rue des Martyrs, 18e
Tel. +33 (0)1 42 52 01 00,
Paris: 33, rue de Grenelle, 7e
Tel. +33 (0)1 42 22 05 07
www.emmanuellezysman.fr

The style

✗ The all-black boutique displays delicate pieces under glass cloches: rings with tiny stones, like ancient pieces from some long-buried treasure, gypsy bracelets with labradorite or black spinel, diamond chokers. Everything is adorable.

LeTéo & Blet

IN A NUTSHELL

It's architect-designed—
hence the fabulous,
structured look!

The style

* Interior architects, designers, and artistic advisors Catherine Le Téo and Thierry Blet are natural-born creatives. Their jewelry collection was launched in 2006. The pieces are in silver or gold, with stylish geometric forms, and each piece tells a story.

The must-have

When each piece is unique and exclusive, everything is a must-have! The boutique is also a must-see, especially the glass atrium.

Paris: 5, rue Casimir-Delavigne, 6ᵉ
Tel. +33 (0)1 43 37 86 84
www.leteoblet.com

Jeanne Danjou et Rousselet

The style

✗ As soon as you step inside this boutique, with its view of the Pont Neuf, you sense that this family—creating costume jewelry since 1920—has seen a great deal of the history of Paris. Here, it's all about Sévigné pearls, with vintage-looking earrings and wonderful rope necklaces at affordable prices. The shop also buys gold jewelry and carries out repairs of all kinds, including reworkings of existing pieces.

The must-have

→ Unbelievably lightweight rope necklaces using cotton or papier-mâché beads.

Paris: 15, place du Pont-Neuf, 1er
Tel. +33 (0)1 43 54 99 32
www.maisonrousselet.com

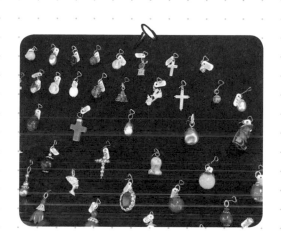

IN A NUTSHELL

Mistinguett used to get her jewelry here—it's the celebs' favorite!

Jérôme Dreyfuss

The style

✱ Ultra-soft, super-practical, with perfect shapes and sizes: Jérôme's bags are every Parisian's wardrobe staple, with a host of clever gizmos like clips for your keys, or an integral mini flashlight to help you rummage on a dark night. Each model has a man's name, and you're sure to fall madly in love very quickly! These are real, everyday bags, bearing the *agricouture* label: Jérôme works with artisans who use traditional vegetable-tanning techniques. The results are beautiful—and organic.

The must-have

⟶ If you haven't got a "Billy," you just haven't understood…

New York: 473 Broome Street
Paris: 1, rue Jacob, 6ᵉ
Tel. +33 (0)1 43 54 70 93
Paris (for the luxury line):
11, rue de l'Échaudé, 6ᵉ
Tel. +33 (0)1 56 24 46 75
www.jerome-dreyfuss.com

Nessim Attal

> ## IN A NUTSHELL
>
> To think some people
> go all the way
> to Saint-Tropez
> for theirs!

The style

✳ A traditional shoemaker, where the owner offers open-toed sandals to measure, in the leather of your choice. The same goes for children, who can even choose to have their Spartan sandals in fluorescent pink. Of course, the shop is packed as soon as the temperature rises, and the waiting list fills up quickly. Best to order your sandals in December.

The must-have

⟶ Your choice—you're the designer!

For globe-trotters, but international orders available by phone!
Paris: 122, rue d'Assas, 6ᵉ
Tel. +33 (0)1 46 34 52 33

Minuit moins 7

The style

✗ Have your luxury shoes repaired by a real pro, accustomed to working with the finest footwear. He can even replace your worn-out red Louboutin soles with brand new ones approved by Christian L. himself! A quintessentially Parisian address, sure to become a favorite pit-stop for American Louboutin fans.

O IN A NUTSHELL

i'll take some more of their homemade shoe polish!

O

BROSSE POUR DAIM
EN CREPE   9€50
SOIE/LAITON   4€50

Paris: 10, passage Véro-Dodat, 1ᵉʳ
Tel. +33 (0)1 42 21 15 47
(for orders, too)
cordonnerie@minuitmoins7.fr

The style

✳ Chic, roots, and rock'n'roll. 58 m is a multi-brand boutique selling shoes and bags by Jérôme Dreyfuss, Avril Gau, K. Jacques, Lanvin, or Alexis Mabille: a perfect selection.

IN A NUTSHELL

Tonight, I'm shopping from their website. Ordering shoes at midnight is so twenty-first century!

The must-have

⟶ A bag or shoes from Tila March, the wildly successful small-scale label created by *Elle* fashion editor Tamara Taichman.

Paris: 58, rue Montmartre, 2ᵉ
Tel. +33 (0)1 40 26 61 01
www.58m.fr

Roger Vivier

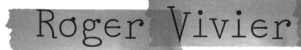

IN A NUTSHELL

i'll have a pair of Catherine Deneuve's. Not the ones she wore in *Belle de Jour*, the ones she designed for Roger Vivier!

The must-have

→ Ballet flats with buckles suit everybody. You can wear them 24/7, with a dress or pants. Genuine chic classics!

The style

✶ "Beautiful things can always go together with style," said Roger Vivier, the master himself. Hence his mix of classic and avant-garde. His timeless ballet flats with buckles ride the vagaries of fashion in regal style—ever since the model was created by Vivier for the coronation of Queen Elizabeth II. For me, the shop is home sweet home.

Bal Harbour, FL: 9700 Collins Avenue
London: 188–189 Sloane Street
New York: 750 Madison Avenue
Paris: 29, rue du Faubourg
Saint-Honoré, 1er
Tel. +33 (0)1 53 43 00 85
www.rogervivier.com

Upla

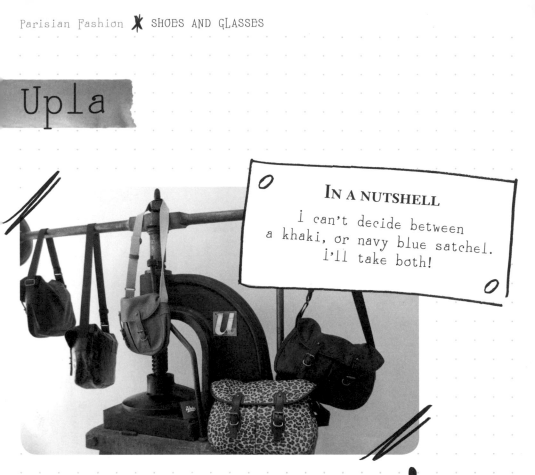

IN A NUTSHELL

I can't decide between a khaki, or navy blue satchel. I'll take both!

The style

✗ Casual bags for that school-girl look. Everyone thinks the brand is English, but it was created in Paris in 1973, in Les Halles.

The must-have

⟶ The fisherman's satchel in a host of colors.

Paris: 5, rue Saint-Benoît, 6ᵉ
Tel. +33 (0)1 40 15 10 75
www.upla.fr

E.B. Meyrowitz

IN A NUTSHELL

You don't need glasses to see how genuinely friendly and competent they are here. Nothing like the frames superstores you find on every street corner.

The must-have

→ The steel glasses-case stamped with the house logo. So popular there's a waiting-list.... I've already got mine, phew!

The style

✳ Haute couture frames: E. B. Meyrowitz makes models to measure. Near place Vendôme, the boutique, opened in 1922, offers exclusive, super-stylish models like Slack by Olivier Lapidus, designed especially for the shop.

Paris: 5, rue de Castiglione, 1er
Tel: +33 (0)1 42 60 63 64
orders: meyerowitz@meyerowitz.com
www.meyrowitz.com

Causse

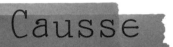

The style

✱ First, when you're telling people about your Causse leather gloves, be sure to point out that they're made at the workshop in Millau, in France, not factory-produced: you'll be singled out as a connoisseur of exceptional craftsmanship. The style is as timeless as their methods— although lately some of the designs incorporate studs....

IN A NUTSHELL

Jackie Kennedy wore Causse gloves.

The must-have

⟶ Elbow-length gloves: the finishing touch for an evening dress.

Paris: 12, rue de Castiglione, 1er
Tel. +33 (0)1 49 26 91 43
www.causse-gantier.fr

Binôme

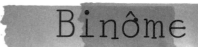

The style

✱ Jewelry designer Delphine Behin and leather accessory designer Delphine Conty created this delightful small boutique to cater to all tastes, at affordable prices. Delphine and Delphine are a friendly and welcoming pair, and their shop is open to other brands too: Hartford, Laurence Doligé, or Des Petits Hauts.

IN A NUTSHELL

The perfect multi-brand store for Parisians who hate bling!

The must-have

⟶ Anything by the two Delphines: always original and exclusive.

Paris: 5, rue de Condé, 6ᵉ
Tel. +33 (0)1 43 25 37 95

PARIS EXCLUSIVE

Le Bon Marché

The style

✱ The quintessence of Left Bank style in one super-stylish department store. From Vanessa Bruno to Balenciaga, and from APC to Lanvin, here are all the latest must-haves. Plus an ultra-hip cosmetics section, a "chic" bookstore, a thoroughly designer home decoration department, and incredible haberdashery, children's toys ("Les 3 hiboux"), and cafés (the most recently opened is Le Miyou, captained by Michelin-starred chef Guy Martin, where you may want to pitch a tent). The perfect destination when you only have a day to shop in Paris. Like Holly Golightly, who spends her days at Tiffany's, it feels like nothing bad can ever happen in the Bon Marché. Especially in the lingerie section, where the changing-rooms offer an interphone link to the sales assistants …

The must-have

⟶ You can shop here with your eyes closed and be sure to come away with something fabulous. Everything has been carefully chosen by some of the finest buyers in Paris.

Paris: 24, rue de Sèvres, 7ᵉ
Tel. +33 (0)1 44 39 80 00
www.lebonmarche.com

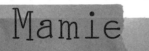

Mamie

The style

✳ Retro, of course—this is a vintage store, an Aladdin's cave of delights to be enjoyed at leisure, breathing in the atmosphere of Old Paree (which includes the owner, a local fixture and friend to everyone from visiting hipsters to old ladies with shopping bags alike—they all stop by for a chat outside the store). There's an incredible selection: I've made some real finds in the bag section. And I've been tempted by the print dresses, too. I was even shown an old pair of Ines de la Fressange shoes: this store really sells the best!

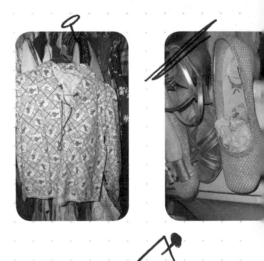

The must-have

⟶ Everything is unique, so take your pick from a truly incredible selection.

Paris: 73, rue de Rochechouart, 9ᵉ
Tel. +33 (0)1 42 82 09 98
www.mamie-vintage.com

IN A NUTSHELL

All the top designers come to buy inspirational items here. Look at these '50s shoes—you can bet they'll be on the runway next season!

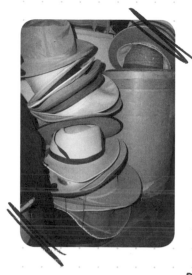

Au petit Matelot

IN A NUTSHELL

i might tell Kate Moss about this place.

The style

✱ The address you'll always want to keep to yourself, because so few people know about it, and you're sure to find what you're after. As the name suggests, seafaring clothes are the order of the day. This is where I find the navy-blue caps I put on in the morning when I haven't had time to do my hair, and what I wear in summer when I want to look like a local by the sea.

The must-have

➔ The perfectly cut fisherman's sweaters.

Paris: 27, avenue de la Grande-Armée, 16ᵉ
Tel. +33 (0)1 45 00 15 51 (for orders, too)

PARIS EXCLUSIVE

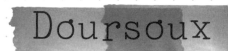

Doursoux

IN A NUTSHELL

Don't tell anyone,
but designers never
succeed in imitating this
stuff, it's already perfect!

The style

* The Mecca for military
clothing. Whenever army style
is back in fashion, this is *the* place:
the combat pants are 100%
original, the military jackets
are unbeatable for quality, and the
men's watches are to die for.

The must-have:

→ The pea coat—indestructible.

Paris: 3, passage Alexandre, 15ᵉ
Tel. +33 (0)1 43 27 00 97
www.doursoux.com

Gotta have it
(but want to stay *chez moi*)

⟶ A Parisian will always find time for a quick spot of shopping, whether on her lunch break ... or just before going to bed. In her (Petit Bateau) nightie, mouse in hand, she can click and shop to her heart's content. If the twenty-first century can't offer us 24/7 shopping, then what? Here's my list of top sites. Baskets at the ready!

www.victoriassecret.com

✖ For a sexy complement to her Petit Bateau underwear, the Parisian orders push-up bras from the USA.

www.topshop.com

✖ No need to fight it out in Top Shop any more! Skip to the front of the line by shopping at Topshop.com.

www.americanapparel.net

✖ A wardrobe essential. No-logo basics in organic cotton, in every color and shape, for the entire family. Order online for the widest selection—or head for your nearest store.

www.rondini.fr

✖ Parisians slip into sandals all summer long, at home and away. The chic thing is to buy them in person, down in St-Trop', from M. Rondini himself, scattering talc on the shoes before you try them on. But we don't all have a yacht in the harbor. Thank heaven for online ordering!

www.urbanoutfitters.com

✖ Funky T-shirts, boho clothes, and a host of witty, kitsch accessories.

www.rustyzipper.com

✖ The e-temple of vintage with thousands of pieces from the 1940s to the 1980s. Rumored to be an inspirational site for top designers.

Hot tips online

⟶ **Two terrific, fun sites for the latest on what's hip and happening in Paris:**

www.doitinparis.com

Everything you ever wanted to know about hip Paris and top addresses in the French capital.

www.mylittleparis.com

For fashion and the latest that's hip—food, hotels, culture, and little luxuries....

www.shopbop.com

✳ Because the Parisian loves to wear brands no one's heard of—this is the ideal place to find new, small-scale US brands, plus fashion greats, with over one hundred labels on the site.

www.abercrombie.com

✳ For everyday sportswear and perfectly cut tanks.

E-sales

⟶ **The Parisian's favorites for bargain-hunting:**

www.theoutnet.com

✳ More than two hundred ultra-chic brands, discounted up to 60%. Not to mention one-off sales where you can get a high-end label at a bargain-basement price.

www.yoox.com

✳ One of the first sites to sell clothes from previous collections, today Yoox is a small empire. I love Yooxygen, the section devoted to eco-design.

www.garancedore.fr

✳You can easily get addicted to Garance's blog. Photos of street looks, illustrations, editorials; the pretty française divides her time between Paris and New York, always pinpointing the best styles to copy.

Chic surfing

⟶ Stay connected with the latest trends—surf these chic sites in your spare moments:

www.net-a-porter.com

✳ Nothing but hip labels and a handful of limited editions. Parisians love the online magazine, always one step ahead of the game.

www.colette.fr

✳ Impossible to talk about Paris without talking about Colette! All the latest happening must-haves you need to know about.

www.luisaviaroma.com

✳ An Italian multi-brand site. A great source of exclusives by designers working for the shop, and no one else.

You want it? You got it!

⟶ What Parisian has never dreamed of owning a genuine Hermès accessory?

Now it's easy! Go to **www.hermes.com** (a charming, brilliant site that's well worth a visit), download a paper version of the object of your desire, paste it together, and *voilà*! Your very own Kelly, or a dog-collar bracelet, in paper form.

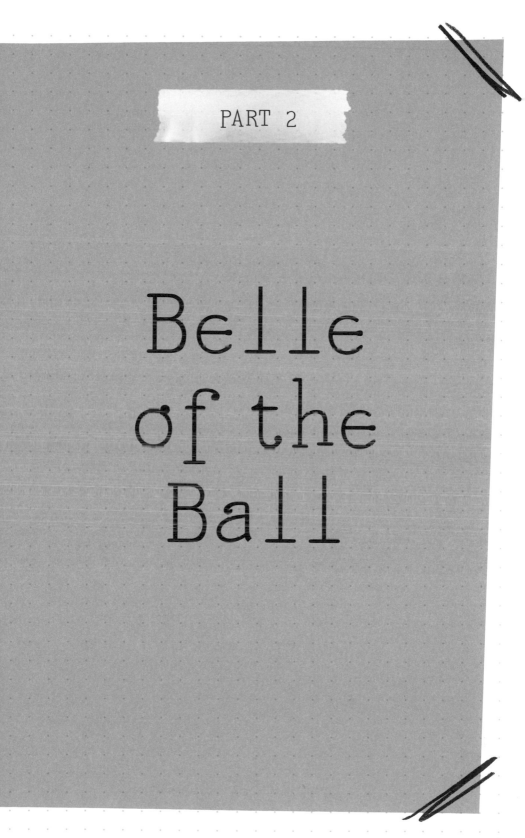

PART 2

Belle of the Ball

1. Beauty Tips

The Parisian loves talking about beauty, but hates spending hours in front of her bathroom mirror. She is not a devotee of multiple masks and day creams, preferring a healthy application of natural good sense … and, of course, these top ten tips.

✳ The Parisian is happy to retouch her makeup during the day with a dab of powder from her compact (always on hand). But she might just as easily forget. And when a tired face rings alarm bells during the evening, there is just one solution—it's time to get some sleep!

✳ The most important beauty routine of all? Makeup removal! And deep cleansing, even without makeup. Makeup in bed is strictly forbidden.

✳ Never use soap on your face, or too much water. Use a cleansing lotion or milk instead. Your skin will dehydrate far less over the years, as every Parisian knows.

✳ There's nothing worse than preening excessively before going out at night. So yesterday! Far better to look fresh and natural by night, and well made-up when you step out in the morning.

✳ The 20-something Parisian scrutinizes her complexion daily in a magnifying mirror; the 50-something Parisian, never. Past a certain age, your overall appeal is far more important. And always be sure your look still rocks!

✳ Never use pink on your lips. Transparent gloss is always best.

✳ Some shampoos are clearly better than others, but how you dry your hair—and what you eat—is far more important. (I've just kissed goodbye to my product endorsement prospects...!)

✳ Don't go bankrupt buying expensive face creams—the best beauty parlor is your local dentist. An attractive smile and great teeth are the best way to forgive and forget the rest!

✳ Avoid over-aggressive professional scrubs and peelings. A stroll with your fiancé in the direction of Tiffany's is the best shortcut to a radiant complexion (and the air is just right inside—very good for the skin)!

✳ Wear makeup every day, even on weekends. Your family wants to see you at your best, too!

2. The Price of Beauty

I like the things I use every day to be
beautiful and so I often choose creams
by their packaging. I never buy makeup
in ugly containers. I love pretty boxes
and stylish bottles and tubes in my
bathroom—they're decorative, and they
always put me in a good mood!

Beauty essentials

→ **Throw out everything else, but be sure to keep these!**

Serge Lutens eye shadow:
→ the packaging is gorgeous, and the texture melts magically on the skin.

Chanel lip gloss:
→ always looks fresher than lipstick.

Elizabeth Arden's Eight Hour Cream:
→ a legendary treatment that makes the rounds backstage at every runway show.

Terracotta moisturizing tan powder from Guerlain:
→ the most effective way to a healthy, sunny complexion. Why go to the Bahamas when you can shop at Guerlain?

INDISPENSABLE

A good toothbrush

It sounds obvious, but I am always surprised by how many people have yellow teeth.

---

memo

Everyone looks better with a little makeup!

Guerlain mascara:
→ Without mascara, I look like a dead fish. Guerlain's tubes are miniature sculptures. I keep one at home and one in the office. I apply to the top lashes only; mascara on the lower lashes can look severe.

Chanel compact foundation:
→ to keep in your bag. An even complexion is essential — which is why almost every woman needs great foundation.

Dior's apricot nail cream:
→ I apply it last thing at night before sleep. It keeps the cuticles perfectly moisturized. The next best thing to a professional manicure!

Neutrogena body oil:
→ penetrates the skin by magic, leaving no oily traces. Of course, it leaves your skin silky-soft, as he will no doubt tell you….

My 10-minute beauty routine

memo

HAVE THREE MAKE-UP BAGS—one for home, one for your bag, one for the office. I do, even if I always forget to refresh my makeup during the day.

REPLACE YOUR MAKEUP REGULARLY: no need to keep that fuchsia lipstick once you've stopped using it, and you don't need a kit worthy of a professional makeup artist.

✳ Wash your hair every morning (it helps you wake up). Apply mousse to wet hair for volume, or a supermarket volume rinse.

✳ I never go out without day cream! I buy mine at the drugstore, and I often change brands. Don't use too much, or your cheek will stick when you greet friends *à la française*.

✳ Use a liquid foundation (a pump-action bottle is easier when you're in a hurry). I keep my foundation compact in my bag for re-touching throughout the day. Warning—never apply foundation with a sponge; use your fingers instead, as for a cream. The result is more natural.

⟶ No time for under eye concealer!

✳ Apply matte powdered eye shadow with a fine brush. I prefer shades of brown, but the choice is yours! One thing is certain—natural colors give a natural look.

⟶ If I have time, I smudge a fine line of black kohl along the base of the lashes.

⟶ Apply a bronzing powder with a big brush.

✳ Apply mascara to the top lashes only—there's no danger of it running during the day.

Scent of a woman

🍃 **I change my perfume every ten years.** I don't like trendy perfumes, which I find often too aggressive. I prefer older, classic brands.

🍃 **When you buy a perfume, test it on your skin, not a strip of paper.** Define your initial choice using the paper strips, then test on the inside of your wrist, leave the shop and wear for a few hours before deciding whether it's worthy of your bathroom shelf.

🍃 **Perfumes shouldn't be treated like trendy clothes.** Even if some perfumes become best-sellers calculated to appeal to everyone, choose a scent to match your personality. The Parisian never leaves a super-fashionable fragrance in her wake, preferring to cross town for that rare, individual essence!

🍃 **Never wear too much perfume; you'll give your friends a headache.** Dab your body's best scent spots: the neck and wrists, but also the ankles and behind the knees for maximum effect. Remember to keep an emergency bottle in your car.

Three beauty secrets

FOR GLOSSY HAIR
Pour three soup spoons of white vinegar diluted in a bowl of water evenly over wet hair after shampooing. Guaranteed to gleam under the flash!

✳

DRINK CARROT JUICE
It tastes good, makes us happy, makes us beautiful—logical!

✳

FOR A DAZZLING SMILE
Use plaque disclosing tablets (from the pharmacy) to locate where you need to improve your brushing technique.

3. Timeless Beauty

My absolute role model is singer Julio Iglesias. Asked if he was afraid of getting old, he replied "But I'm already old…" The Parisian is more worried about wrinkles at 20 than she is at 50.

memo

Frivolity is the key
to eternal youth!

I pay no attention to wrinkles, I just stand back from the mirror!
I'll try Botox when I see a result I like…. To date, it always looks to me as if something has gone wrong. The Parisian embraces the advantages of age: she knows how to pack one suitcase instead of four. She lives for the present. She listens. She puts things in perspective. But aging doesn't mean letting yourself go. These are my personal beauty tips.

For lifelong beauty:

✳ Be well-groomed.

✳ Smell nice.

✳ Look after your teeth. Have them professionally cleaned every six months.

✳ Smile.

✳ Be indulgent.

✳ Be nonchalant and forget your age.

✳ Be cooler and more easy-going.

✳ Be less selfish.

✳ Be passionate about a man, a project, a house. It's an instant facelift.

✳ Do only what suits you. The perfect Zen attitude.

✳ Accept that there will be bad days. And make the most of the good days!

Plus:

✱ Moisturize your skin thoroughly.

✱ Use mascara, but forget liquid eyeliner.

✱ Choose foundation that's slightly paler than your natural tone. It will soften your complexion and even out dark shadows.

✱ Choose a bright lipstick, or gloss.

✱ Keep your nails short and manicure them regularly.

Perfect make-up at 50+:

⟶ If your eyes are made up, leave your skin pale and natural.

⟶ If your eyes are *au naturel*, give your skin a warm foundation.

⟶ Don't shine, but don't look as if you've used-up your entire powder puff, either.

memo

**An hour sleeping
or making love
is better than
a Botox injection
at the dermatologist's.**

Things to avoid at all cost (or you'll look ten years older):

● Too much heavy, opaque foundation, especially if it's too dark (*à la* "I'm a tanning salon regular").

● Glittery eye shadow—will only make your wrinkles sparkle....

● Thick, neglected eyebrows.

● Too much powder.

● Brown blush in the hollows of your cheeks.

● A contour line around the lips

● Sparkly orange or "nude" lipstick.

... all these things will make you look far older than you really are!

4. Beauty Faux Pas

As with fashion, we can all make beauty mistakes. Make-up trends are unimportant—it's all a question of harmonizing with your natural physiognomy and complexion. Runway models may sport blue false eyelashes, invisible eyebrows, or metallic blusher, but we live in the real world, minus spotlights and flash photography. Even a supermodel looks her best *au naturel*. Here's what to avoid if you don't want to look like a "makeup victim".

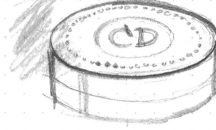

✳ **Blusher applied like war paint.** War is over…

✳ **Sparkly, shimmery, glittery makeup.** Off the runway or fashion magazine pages, it's off limits.

✳ **Makeup to match your clothes—you'll look like a girl who thinks too hard and really shouldn't.** Have faith in your natural complexion, eye, and hair color instead.

✳ **Too much cover-up and foundation** (you'll look ashen-faced).

✳ **Foundation applied too quickly, without going right up to the hairline.** The mask unmasked!

✳ **Overly plucked eyebrows.** Afterwards, you're tempted to draw in the missing hairs with a pencil—never a good idea!

✳ **Too much eyeliner** (a.k.a. the "raccoon" look).

✳ **Inexpertly applied "smoky eyes"** (a.k.a. the "panda" look). Never attempt effects you haven't mastered.

✳ **Colored lip contours.** Never very attractive. Especially if darker than your lip color.

✳ **Under-arm hair.** Parisians spend a great deal on epilation (as a rule, the Parisian male dislikes body hair).

✳ **Blue eye shadow.** A wrong turn if you're in search of a natural look!

✳ **Glittery eye shadow on the eyes.** Makes even the most youthful skin look old.

✳ **Mascara on the lower lashes—** it hardens your gaze and accentuates dark circles under the eyes.

✳ **Too much lip gloss.** Your mouth will look sticky—not attractive.

PART 3

Chez Moi

1. The Parisian Home

The Parisian's (often small) apartment
is her château! An over-arching theme is
the best way to add a distinctive, stylish touch,
whether it's based on a color scheme, a genre,
or a period. Compose your own home style
book using magazine photographs, to help
define your personal look.

⟶ I like to make changes when it comes to decoration. My last apartment was quite traditional and full of ornaments. My current place is more minimalist designer chic. A regular change of decor gives your home a facelift—nothing is more depressing than watching your furniture grow old with you! Of course, there's no need for sweeping alterations: a few clever touches are all that's required. Think "incoming First Lady" and make small, inexpensive, but significant changes for maximum effect!

Respect your home's essential charm and character.

The Parisian dresses to suit her personal style and shape, and the same goes for decoration: always respect your home's essential style and sense of place. For a funky look in a period apartment, try painting the ceiling moldings rose pink (destroying period moldings is a crime in central Paris).

Your decor should reflect your personality.

There are two sides to mine: I love uncluttered Zen style, but I also love traditional folk and tribal art. Don't decorate your apartment like a period film set: anachronisms are allowed! As with fashion, don't hesitate to mix it up. IKEA furniture, designer pieces, and flea-market finds can live together in harmony. I have no problem placing an IKEA sofa alongside '60s designer lamps and a repainted bookshelf from the Marché aux Puces. Remember: for fashion and decor alike, the "total look" is out.

Box it up!

A great solution for small spaces. Parisians collect zinc boxes and arrange them on shelves (Muji is a favorite hunting-ground: www. muji.com). Piled high and clearly labeled (candles, shoe-cleaning kit, light bulbs, sewing materials, etc.) they're guaranteed to help you find everything at the drop of a hat.

Make your own works of art.

Why pay a fortune for original art in your home? Put your favorite children's drawings under glass with a silver craft paper mount. I love anything drawn by small children— the under-10s express themselves so freely, with great talent, which they lose as they grow. I give children sheets of drawing paper and charcoal pencils, and they come up with fabulous artwork just waiting to be framed! Objects look great framed, too. I use made-to-measure Plexiglas boxes from Gypel in Paris (9, rue Jean-Jacques-Rousseau, 1er. Tel. +33 [0]1 42 36 15 79). Magnetic Plexiglas frames (Muji again) can transform a simple scribbled message into a work of art. The same goes for your favorite magazine photographs: cut them out and frame them. There is no such thing as a "lesser art".

What's cooking

STORE KITCHEN UTENSILS IN POTS AND VASES

Finding new uses for existing objects is always fun. As with fashion, an offbeat approach to decorating is the key.

MAKE A STATEMENT WITH STYLISH TABLEWARE

I love square plates with rounded corners, like my kitchen table. They're hard to find, but so much more original than round or square ones!

Think white.

OK, I have a bright rose pink office wall (it gives off a superb light, and gives everyone a fresh complexion) but for small apartments, I recommend white. As a general rule, if you're hesitating between two colors, go for white. A careful choice of color can transform a small space into a stylish loft: a range of gray, beige, khaki, and touches of black. And if you're currently experiencing a blue, pink, or green period, try a single wall of color rather than the total look—you can always change it a few months later.

Place scented candles in each room.

A nice smell is as important as great furniture. Light them as soon as you come home, even if it isn't dark.

Hide unsightly objects.

For example, keep your depressing gray printer in a cupboard. Simple!

make a splash in the bath

BASIC BATH TOWELS ARE BEST

It's easy to get carried away in the store by a stunning turquoise towel, beckoning like an enticing tropical lagoon. But be warned—it may not match your tiles back at home (turquoise tiles are seldom a good idea anyway). My advice: stick to one or two bathroom colors. All my towels are plain black or white. I order them online from the French catalog *La Redoute* (see their AMPM collection at www.ampm.fr or www.laredoute.co.uk). I never tire of them, and I'm sure to find replacements when they show signs of wear, unlike "turquoise lagoon," which is not a staple.

STYLISH SOAP

Decant your handwash—avoid horrible plastic bottles with flashy logos. Pour the contents into your own plain glass or ceramic dispenser. The same goes for tissues: hide them in boxes that match your decor.

Keep it simple—curtain rods.

A simple wrought-iron rod is worth any number of faux Louis XVI versions. For ultimate simplicity, avoid curtains altogether.

Keep it simple—lights.

Avoid overly complicated designs in favor of simple, practical spotlights. A single designer lamp can make a strong statement.

Use a striking sofa or armchair to make a "statement".

A little like a well-chosen fashion accessory—it's worth investing in a "name" here. A strong statement can set the tone in a minimalist decor. Statement lamps are another highly effective option.

Display fruit.

When your fruit basket overflows with oranges and apples, put them in clear glass vases—pretty and practical.

Cover your sofa and armchairs with fabric throws.

Two advantages: it minimizes wear and tear (I have dogs!) and you can change your decor easily and inexpensively.

Add a touch of humor.

With glasses shaped liked plastic cups (find in them in Paris at Galerie Sentou www.sentou.fr). An element of surprise is always welcome!

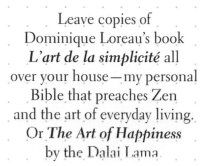

Leave copies of Dominique Loreau's book *L'art de la simplicité* all over your house—my personal Bible that preaches Zen and the art of everyday living. Or *The Art of Happiness* by the Dalai Lama

minimize clutter.

A thorough Spring cleaning costs nothing, and an apartment devoid of surplus objects and dust is so much more chic. Plus, parting with objects you thought mattered can be highly beneficial! I no longer feel the need to accumulate baubles picked up at flea-markets (once a favorite activity). The (difficult) trick is to create a small corner of cheerful clutter, strategically positioned to counterbalance your minimalist decor; an elegant atmosphere should never feel stuffy or serious—a much-loved children's toy under Plexiglas in the middle of your living room should do the trick!

THE GOLDEN RULE FOR SMALL SPACES

A small space must be tidy to be inhabitable!
My apartment covers 750 square feet (large for the center of Paris) but I'm not the only person who lives there. Storage is essential, and every possible corner of space is used (under the sloping attic ceilings, under the bed, under the stairs). Find clever double uses for your objects—I store my dogs' food in a chest that doubles as a bench.

Flower power

→ **Ugly bouquets exist!
You won't go wrong if you:**

✳ Include white orchids,
the favorite of design aficionados.

✳ Choose a long-stemmed, colored
flower (a peony, for example) displayed
on its own in a slender "test-tube"
vase. Several times over.

✳ Opt for an all-white bouquet
(never fails).

✳ Fill your house with plants.
Especially if they're in black
or zinc pots.

Best to avoid:

✳ Multicolored floral bouquets:
choose three colors at the very most
(even then, your third color should
be white!).

✳ Chrysanthemums are a forbidden
flower, especially in France,
where they are traditionally placed
on tombs.

✳ Very long-stemmed flowers. Very
difficult to find a suitable vase.

Or customize:

✳ If your friend's or admirer's
bouquet is truly hideous, divide and
conquer! Several small posies will
always look better.

2. The Perfect Closet

A well-organized closet can be the key
to a whole new outlook on life. Tiny Parisian
apartments don't lend themselves to walk-in
dressing areas, and keeping everything tidy
can be a challenge. I don't advise throwing
everything out for lack of space (but be
honest, will you ever wear that 1980s mohair
sweater again?), so here are seven ways to
organize your space.

Know how to "edit" your wardrobe.

✳ "Editing" is so much classier and more professional than "getting rid of," but it means exactly the same thing. Clear out anything in poor condition and unworn for ages. If you look at something and don't plan to wear it soon, out it goes. Can't decide? Think of a friend whose style you admire and ask, would she wear this? If the answer is no, ruthless editing is the solution!

Categorize your clothes!

✳ Pants with pants, T-shirts all together, sweaters to one side, etc. Separate your clothes by season, and for top marks, sort them by color. Your closet will look wonderful every time you open the door.

Invest in a single type of clothes hanger.

✳ Try the plain black or white plastic ones from IKEA, which take up no space and are ideal for hanging anything and everything.
Unification = organization.

Give everything a front row seat.

✳ Not always easy, but if you can't see things, you won't wear them.

Organize your jewelry and accessories in Plexiglas boxes

✳ with drawers (Muji). It's so much easier to choose when you can see everything.

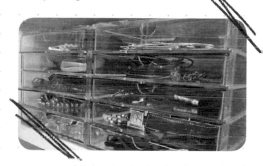

Photograph your shoes.

✳ Take Polaroid or digital snaps of your shoes and glue them to the outside of their boxes, then pile them up shoe store-style. If you don't have enough space, store several pairs in larger boxes.

My secret luxury.

✳ I still make room for "hideous clothes I just have to keep" and "fabulous things that are so *not* my style but I love anyway." This is the key to a happy "closet" relationship! But if you really don't have space, out they go....

3. Parisian Deco

Shop in Paris... or Online

Merci

An amazing, original range. The 16,150-square-foot store offers everything from costly items (the furniture collection) to more everyday objects (clever designer kitchen accessories). There are exclusive collections of clothes from big-name designers, multi-colored crayons, vintage notebooks, plus small haberdashery and hardware sections, jewelry, and a perfume lab courtesy of Goutal. Even a florist. The result is eclectic and oh-so-Parisian! For a food break, visit the ground-floor restaurant, serving delicious salads and cakes so good you'd get up in the middle of the night to eat them. Shopaholics are free to indulge, safe in the knowledge that part of the profits are donated to a fund for underprivileged children.

Merci, Merci!

Paris: 11, boulevard Beaumarchais, 3ᵉ
Tel. +33 (0)1 42 77 00 33
www.merci-merci.com

E-deco

www.laredoute.co.uk

The decoration section of French catalog *La Redoute*. For washed linen sheets and bath towels (I order them in black). Furniture, too—well worth a click!

www.madeindesign.co.uk

Definitely one to include in your personal list of favorites. A completely comprehensive range, for every pocket. Their absolute must? The Luxembourg chair by designer Frédéric Sofia for Fermob: the same as the ones in the Jardin du Luxembourg.

www.fab.com

Buy direct online—the site sells furniture at outlet prices. You can buy in advance from upcoming collections, or secure your own limited edition piece. The factories (often based in China) will deliver direct, but allow several months. That's the price of budget shopping online!

www.atylia.fr

The perfect e-address for stylish, small gifts. Order outside France by phone : +33 (0)1 45 06 71 16.

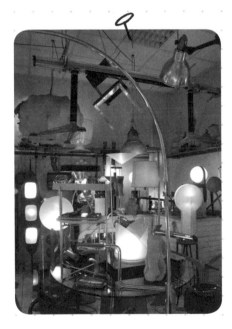

Paris's top vintage lamp store

Complément d'objet

A truly fabulous address for
essential home accessories,
selling lamps of all kinds,
from brilliant basics to ultra-rare
pieces, and lamps guaranteed to
transport you straight back
to childhood. From the 1930s
to the 1990s, with a huge stock
of 1960s designs, this is a dazzling
Aladdin's cave!

Paris: 11, rue Jean-Pierre-Timbaud, 11ᵉ
Tel. +33 (0)1 43 57 09 28
www.complementdobjet.com

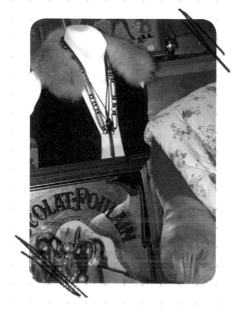

Paris's top radiator shop

WorldStyle Design

OK, radiators don't draw the biggest crowds, but this place is a magnet for style-conscious Parisians—every piece is a design classic! An address to treasure—designer radiators are few and far between!

Paris: 203 bis, boulevard Saint-Germain, 7ᵉ
Tel. +33 (0)1 40 26 92 80
www.worldstyle.com

Paris's top bric-a-brac shop

Hétéroclite

When you go into this shop, you get the sense that you've entered another dimension. This truly charming jumble of objects, scouted up by friendly Dominique, plunges us into a wonderland where anyone who looks carefully can come away with a treasure. Lots of furniture, wonderful jewelry, toys for tots, and a plethora of vintage items; an authentic Parisian antique shop.

111, rue de Vaugirard, 6ᵉ
Tel. +33 (0)1 45 48 44 51

PARIS EXCLUSIVE

Paris's top sofa store

Caravane Chambre 19

I couldn't live without this store! Unbeatable for well-designed sofas, Caravane also offers a host of other pieces and decorative objects in a distinctive—and addictive—exotic-contemporary-Parisian style. There are two boutiques in Paris's 12⁰ arrondissement: one sells small items, tableware, and fabrics, the other furniture and beds. This is my favorite place in the world for home decoration, naturally enough given that the store is the brainchild of decoration guru and *grande dame* Françoise Dorget. Her mix of styles is the last word in sophistication. Visit the shop for inspiration and you'll be running home to recreate it from top to bottom. I never tire of her magnificent fabrics to use as sofa throws. Caravane's best-seller? The Thala sofa with removable covers. Sit down, and you'll never want to get up. An exotic, cosmopolitan, urban, oh-so-Parisian store.

Paris: 19 and 22, rue Saint-Nicolas, 12ᵉ
Tel. + 33 (0)1 53 02 96 96
6, rue Pavée, 4ᵉ
Tel. + 33 (0)1 44 61 04 20
www.caravane.fr

Paris's top storage store

Muji

Yes, the brand is Japanese, but their minimalist style goes with everything! I'm a boxaholic—I collect them, pile them up, and dot them around my apartment. (I actually keep things in them, too). Muji is storage heaven. Everything is plain and understated: transparent, white, wicker, or steel. Impossible to go wrong!

London: 157 Kensington High Street
New York: 620 Eigth Street.
Paris: 30, rue Saint-Sulpice, 6ᵉ
Tel. +33 (0)1 44 07 37 30
www.muji.us and www.mujionline.co.uk

Paris's top shop for "déco statements"

Galerie Sentou

My kind of design. A selection of fine pieces, and a host of charming small gifts from Tsé & Tsé and Roger Tallon, plus the shop's own range, guaranteed to blend with your style and ring the changes all at once.

Paris: 26, boulevard Raspail, 7ᵉ
Tel. +33 (0)1 45 49 00 05
Paris: 29, rue François-Miron, 4ᵉ
Tel. +33 (0)1 42 78 50 60
www.sentou.fr (many products also available from madeindesign.co.uk)

Paris's top store for chic, fun furniture

La Maison Darré

Vincent Darré is one of my dearest friends, who worked in fashion before launching into the wonderful world of art furniture. He has limitless imagination, and his boutique is an offbeat laboratory for new objects and furniture with a distinctive mix of exuberant fun and rigorous design. Like his *Vertèbres* chair or the *bureau des vanités* with bone legs. Irresistibly entertaining.

Paris: 32, rue Mont-Thabor, 1er
Tel. + 33 (0)1 42 60 27 97
www.maisondarre.com

Paris's top frame store

Gypel

Guaranteed to present any object, photograph, or painting to the best possible effect. Full of good ideas to help you achieve the desired look—a decoration must.

Paris: 9, rue Jean-Jacques-Rousseau, 1er
Tel. +33 (0)1 42 36 15 79

PARIS EXCLUSIVE

Paris's top venue for nostalgic antiques

Mamie Gâteaux

The atmosphere in the antique shop, where everything brings back childhood memories circa 1950, is distinctively nostalgic. The tasteful selection in the adjacent boutique reflects the Japanese owner's "streamlined and authentic" sensibilities (Mariko runs the shop with her husband Hervé): wicker baskets, ultra-simple porcelain bowls, linen bags. At their tearoom just a few doors away you can sample Mariko's homemade cakes, which are simply irresistible (she's a trained pastry chef). You can't say I didn't warn you!

PARIS EXCLUSIVE

66–68–70, rue du Cherche-Midi, 6ᵉ
Tel.: +33 (0)1 45 44 36 63 (boutique and vintage shop) and +33 (0)1 42 22 32 15 (tearoom)

Paris's top stop for photo albums

Bookbinders Design

A black photo album on which we can inscribe a name or a year in silver is decidedly chic. And don't miss the binders for organizing DVDs, which is the best way to exhibit style in a small apartment.

Melbourne, Australia: The Galleria, Shop E25, 385 Bourke Street
Paris: 130, rue du Bac, 7ᵉ
Tel. +33 (0)1 42 22 73 66
www.bookbindersdesign.com

Paris's top stop for European designers.

The Collection

A decoration boutique focusing on European design. Look out for the special editions of pieces made exclusively for the store. Plus Tracy Kendall wallpapers, the Brocante de Salon carpet by Atelier Blink, or Émilie Rabiller's self-adhesive room frieze that you can write on and wipe clean. Visitors quickly become die-hard fans of the whimsical designer atmosphere, and its contents.

Paris: 33, rue de Poitou, 3^e
Tel. + 33 (0)1 42 77 04 20
www.thecollection.fr

Chic galleries

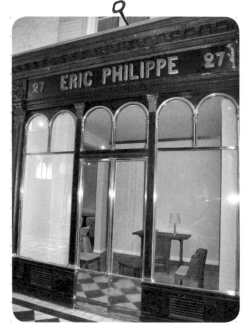

Éric Philippe

Eric Philippe is hidden away in one of Paris's chicest covered arcades. An expert in twentieth-century furniture, he specializes in Scandinavian design from the 1920s to the 1980s, plus American designers of the 1950s. Clean lines and superb style: I love it! Eric offers advice on choosing furniture based on your personal taste. Just ask!

Paris: 25, galerie Véro-Dodat, 1er
Tel. +33 (0)1 42 33 28 26
www.ericphilippe.com

Galerie du Passage

Just opposite Éric Philippe's gallery, the Galerie du Passage recently celebrated its twentieth birthday. Owner Pierre Passebon is world famous for his superb selection of twentieth-century and contemporary furniture and objects. There's always a special exhibition worth a visit. This is a friendly, welcoming showcase for irresistible objects of desire. will you succumb?

Paris: 20–26, galerie Véro-Dodat, 1er
Tel. +33 (0)1 42 36 01 13
www.galeriedupassage.com

Art Up Deco

Artworks from 60€ — a truly seductive concept. I recently bought two superb paintings here, both by young unknown painters, sold supermarket-style at affordable prices. The future of the art market starts here?

Paris: 39, boulevard Malesherbes, 8e
Tel. +33 (0)1 43 36 47 95
www.artupdeco.com

4.Countdown to a Perfect Dinner

Everyone assumes I throw ultra-sophisticated dinners for *le tout Paris*. Not at all! When I entertain at home, I want to spend time with friends, not slave over a hot oven. Here's my personal countdown for a contemporary, informal dinner *à la Parisienne*.

1 hour to go

⟶ Have your children decorate the table – they're full of creative ideas. I lay a colored tablecloth (navy blue is always good) and the children take care of the rest: black plastic plates, unmatched old white china.... Everyone will love it! Homemade table decorations add a perfect arty touch.

2 hours before

⟶ Rush home after work, usually without shopping. Just time to buy chicken on the way. Nothing to wear. Living room a riot of newspapers and children's stuff.

30 minutes to go

⟶ No need for a bewildering array of aperitifs. Nowadays, red and white wine are fine for everyone, *and* you keep your head for the whole evening. For non-drinkers, water and fruit juices are perfect.

90 minutes to go

⟶ Put the chicken in a deep cooking pot with whatever's on hand—peeled tomatoes, chopped onions, herbs and spices (curry, coriander, thyme), and a generous slosh of olive oil. Stir it all up, place on a low heat. While the chicken cooks, tidy up. Take a bath.

They're here

⟶ When guests arrive, I serve sesame bread sticks, cherry tomatoes, and baby vegetables piled into glasses, for a stylish touch. Keep your guests hungry! The longer they wait, the more they'll tell you how delicious everything is.

1½ hours later

⟶ Time to cook the fragrant basmati rice (always an elegant touch). By now, your guests are crowing for food.

after 2 hours

⟶ The chicken is a great success ("*à la* what, did you say?"). One important lesson, from years of experience: people come to your home to spend time with you, not to savor a gourmet meal—leave that to the professionals. And you're not there to parade your Cordon Bleu skills. One of my favorite dinners recently began with the host asking everyone "What would you like on your pizza?"

Then he called the Italian restaurant next door. Here was a man who understood: we were all delighted with our pizzas, and he spent a stress-free evening with friends. If you must roll out the gourmet red carpet, prepare as much as possible in advance.

after 3 hours

⟶ Dessert, and time for a surprise. I like to serve chocolate mousse in miniature dishes, like a doll's tea set. Or a really good ice cream (bought, of course) in quality cones. Much more fun! As with fashion and decor, when it comes to entertaining, less is more. Don't overdo it and the atmosphere will be more relaxed. That gives you time to come out of the kitchen and enjoy entertaining.

TIP

Of course, you can't serve
the same meal ten times over
to the same friends. If, like
me, your only dish is pot-roasted
chicken or pasta (simple—the
instructions are on the packet)
sign up for a cooking course
and learn some fun, simple
recipes. This will also make
a change from sushi ordered
in from your local restaurant.
Cooking classes also make
great gifts—perhaps for
that friend who always serves
pot-roasted chicken?

My favorite cooking school
in Paris?

L'atelier de Fred

Passage de l'Ancre
223, rue Saint-Martin, 3ᵉ
Tel. +33 (0)1 40 29 46 04
www.latelierdefred.com

PARIS EXCLUSIVE

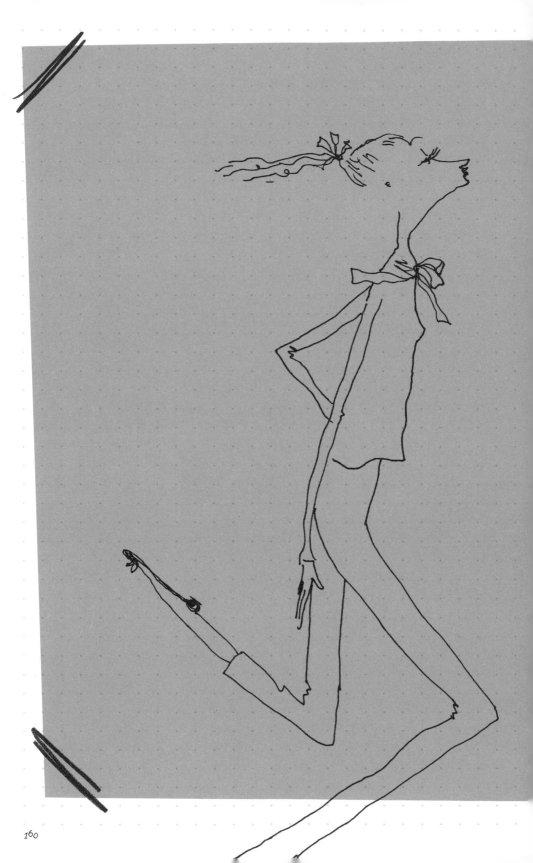

ines's
Paris

1. "Secret" Paris

The true Parisian has a certain style—and a certain way of enjoying her city, exploring offbeat neighborhoods, "secret" museums, quaint and cosmopolitan haunts. Here are some of my favorite things to do, and places to go, plus some handpicked addresses for anyone planning a trip to the city.

Offbeat museums

→ There's the Louvre of course, or the Musée d'Orsay, or the Pompidou. But the true Parisian prefers the city's little-known museums (an intimate knowledge of art venues off the beaten track is *so* chic). Here are four of my favorites.

Musée Dapper

50, avenue Victor-Hugo, 16ᵉ
Tel. + 33 (0)1 45 00 01 50
www.dapper.com.fr

✱ For African art, especially the stunning sculptures. If you want to look like a true art aficionado, say "I'm off to the Musée Dapper, do you know it?" (Because so few people do.) Add, "Their temporary exhibitions are magnificent," to prove you're a regular!

Musée Marmottan Monet

2, rue Louis Boilly, 16ᵉ
Tel. +33 (0)1 42 24 07 02
www.marmottan.com

✱ Devoted to Impressionism, in a lovely private townhouse with its own garden. This is the home of the world's largest collection of works by Claude Monet. Make an impression—tell your friends!

Musée Cognacq-Jay

8, rue Elzévir, 3ᵉ
Tel. +33 (0)1 40 27 07 21

✱ This small art museum is a well-kept secret, even in Paris. There are paintings, sculptures, drawings, furniture, and porcelain, primarily from the eighteenth century. The works were collected by Ernest Cognacq, the founder of the Samaritaine department store. *C'est très Paris*!

Musée Jacquemart-André

158, boulevard Haussmann, 8ᵉ
Tel. +33 (0)1 45 62 11 59
www.musee-jacquemart-andre.com

✱ A private collection amassed by a couple of art lovers who adored everything from Flemish to Italian Renaissance painting, and rare furniture. Just five minutes from the Champs-Elysées, in a building that's well worth a visit in its own right. The tearoom is a veritable work of art, too—one of the chicest in Paris, a place where you can feast your eyes at the same time as your taste buds!

Check out a (nearly) secret spot

→ "Really? You've never heard of it?" The Parisian loves to surprise her friends with tips on places they know nothing about. She is constantly on the hunt for her city's best-kept secrets— until she tells all, and sets off in search of another new discovery.

Best bathrooms

If you really want to surprise a friend on a day out in Paris, stand in front of the Madeleine church with your back to the Concorde obelisk, and look for a small staircase on your right leading down to some public toilets (*mais oui!*). Here is a little-known Belle Epoque gem, all polished wood and ceramics, perfectly preserved but still in working order, as if the secret underground location had kept it safe from "improvements" ordered by the city's municipal councils in decades past. The old-world atmosphere extends to the dedicated, enthusiastic attendant employed to keep the place spotless—straight out of a novel by Marcel Proust! The "time travel" effect is remarkable: this sanitary space is a genuine piece of Old Paris, far more authentic than many tourist sites. Perhaps the toilets are a listed heritage site, perhaps not—what's certain is that very few Parisians know this (convenient) attraction exists!

Toilettes de la Madeleine
Place de la Madeleine, 8ᵉ

Venerable bookshops

→ The Parisian buys plenty of books, but never has time to read them! But these shops specialize in gorgeous art and fashion books, rare editions, prints, and retro magazines; great for perusing and an ideal source for the perfect decorative touch. Here are my favorite atmospheric Paris bookshops, for browsing in style.

Galignani

The first English-language bookshop established in continental Europe, with a fine stock of English (and French) books and magazines. Their fashion section is fabulous; I could spend hours here!

224, rue de Rivoli, 1er
Tel. +33 (0)1 42 60 76 07
www.galignani.com

Librairie F. Jousseaume

In a quiet, covered arcade, with beautiful, natural light. If you love old books, you'll adore this place. Plus a wonderful selection of nineteenth-century fashion plates.

45–47, galerie Vivienne, 2e
Tel. +33 (0)1 42 96 06 24

THE FIRST

ENGLISH BOOKSHOP

ESTABLISHED

ON THE

CONTINENT

Les Archives de la Presse

Vintage magazine heaven—packed with old copies of *Elle* and *Vogue*.

51, rue des Archives, 3ᵉ
www.lesarchivesdelapresse.com

L'Écume des Pages

This cult bookshop in Saint-Germain-des Prés always stocks a selection of the books *le tout Paris* is talking about.

174, boulevard Saint-Germain, 6ᵉ
Tel. +33 (0)1 45 48 54 48
www.ecumedespages.fr

La Librairie des Archives

A mine of great art books, and rare or out-of-print editions.

83, rue Vieille-du-Temple, 3ᵉ
Tel. +33 (0)1 42 72 13 58
www.librairiedesarchives.com

Librairie La Hune

Between the Café de Flore and the Deux-Magots, this is the perfect place to feed on fine literature until late at night (the store closes at midnight from Monday to Saturday, and at 8pm on Sunday). Step inside the immaculate white space, and you're sure to come out with an illuminating book. (Perhaps you can stop by to pick-up another copy of *Parisian Chic* for your best friend?)

170, boulevard Saint-Germain, 3ᵉ
Tel. +33 (0)1 45 48 35 85

International Paris

→ The Parisian likes nothing more than to get away from it all and travel the world, right in the heart of her favorite city! Here are my favorite addresses for a bit of globe-trotting inside the confines of the Paris *périphérique*—and the perfect cure for homesickness should it hit!

Japan

Lô Sushi

8, rue de Berri, 8ᵉ
Tel. +33 (0)1 45 62 01 00
www.losushi.com

🖋 For a quick lunch, this is the perfect solution: there's no waiting, just take a seat at the conveyor belt counter and help yourself. The colored dishes indicate the price of each delicacy. But you can take your time here, too—the setting is super-stylish and very relaxed. Japanese visitors to Paris appreciate the taste of home when they're "lost in translation"—the menu is all in Japanese.

India

La Maison du Kashmir

8, rue Sainte-Beuve, 6ᵉ
Tel. +33 (0)1 45 48 66 06

🖋 You can't mistake the origin of the food here—as soon you step inside, the decor tells you you're not in Nicaragua. A riot of red and pink, curtains trimmed with gold braid, and napkins folded into fans: welcome to India! What to order? The vegetarian thali and sweet lassi are a true taste of the subcontinent.

North Africa

The tearoom at the Paris mosque

39, rue Geoffroy-Saint-Hillaire, 5ᵉ
Tel. +33 (0)1 43 31 18 14

🖋 In summer, you can sit outside in the delightful, small, typically North African courtyard, decorated with colorful mosaics and serving super-sweet mint tea. Assorted pastries are displayed at the counter—traditional treats include delicacies flavored with honey and almonds, and fabulous, evocatively named *cornes de gazelle*. Calorific, but so delicious!

Thailand

Le Comptoir de Thiou

12, avenue Georges-V, 8ᵉ
Tel. 01 47 20 89 56

 The ideal place for lunch if you're shopping in the 8ᵉ. The *Tigre qui pleure* (literally "Weeping Tiger") is a must, as is the Pad Thai. A lemongrass infusion makes the perfect finish to a light, healthy meal.

USA

Coffee Parisien

4, rue Princesse, 6ᵉ
Tel. 33 (0)1 43 54 18 18

 A great American atmosphere with pictures of US presidents on the walls and place mats. This is a wonderful place to bring children for all-American burgers with chunky fries. And for figure-conscious parents, there are delicious salads, too.

Thanksgiving

20, rue Saint-Paul, 4ᵉ
Tel. +33 (0)1 42 77 68 29
www.thanksgivingparis.com

 A grocery store with a truly all-American range, from pancake mix to Paul Newman popcorn, Oreos, and, when Thanksgiving comes around, the biggest turkeys you'll ever see. Upstairs, the Cajun restaurant serves a great brunch.

Great Britain

WH Smith

248, rue de Rivoli, 1ᵉʳ
Tel. +33 (0)1 44 77 88 99
www.whsmith.fr

 On the first floor, a small grocery section sells a range of British products unrivaled almost anywhere else in Paris. Parisians love it for the wonderful selection of children's books in English, English-language DVDs, and British and American magazines.

Italy

Casa Bini

36, rue Grégoire-de-Tours, 6ᵉ
Tel. +33 (0)1 46 34 05 60

 An institution for fine Tuscan cuisine. There's a warm, ultra-Italian welcome, and wonderfully fresh pasta. The decor is somewhat austere, but the clientele is *very* chic! Book ahead: Casa Bini's addicted regulars are very reluctant to make room for newcomers.

2. Family Fun

My out-of-town friends always ask: "But how do you cope with children in Paris?" The answer is simple: Paris offers so many ways to keep them busy, I've never had time to think about it. Museums, parks, bookshops, toyshops, shows, and historic sites- -taking the children out in Paris is always fun!

Bonpoint

You're sure to find whatever you're looking for at Bonpoint, especially at the rue de Tournon boutique, a sublimely beautiful space. The collection caters for babies through to teenagers, in subtle colors with fabulous prints and wonderful easy-chic cuts. A great place for down jackets in winter and pretty Liberty-print dresses or boys' shirts in summer. Their special eau de cologne for babies is the perfect gift for a new arrival. And if the little ones get fidgety while you're shopping (unlikely—there's a log cabin play area) promise them a brownie in the restaurant downstairs, with its own leafy courtyard, one of Paris's best-kept secrets … at least until this book was published!

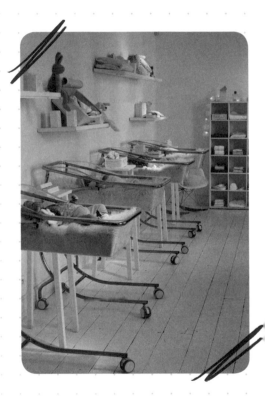

Bal Harbour, FL: 9700 Collins Avenue
Beverly Hills: 9521 Brighton Way
New York: 810 and 1269 Madison Avenue
and 392 Bleeker Street
Palm Beach, FL: 246 Worth Avenue
London: 256 Brompton Road,
15 Sloane Street,
52–54 Marylebone High Street and
197 Westbourne Grove
Paris: 6, rue de Tournon, 6ᵉ
Tel. +33 (0)1 40 51 98 20
www.bonpoint.com

Baudou

The name has changed, but this is still Bonpoint's furniture store—the perfect address for quality children's bedroom furniture in lovely, soft colors, with no irritating, superfluous "cutesy" decorative touches. And if you haven't got space for the furniture, you can buy one of their irresistible teddy bears.

7, rue de Solferino, 7e
Tel. +33 (0)1 45 55 42 79
www.baudoumeuble.com

Zef

Zef's poetic, fairytale atmosphere is inspired by owner Mariu De Andreis's home country of Italy. The star of the show? The starry prints! Everything is delightful, from the neat, delicate dresses to winter coats. The Zef Piccolo collection for newborns is sooooo cute! You'll want it *all*. Impossible to leave this shop without buying something—you have been warned!

15, rue Debelleyme, 3ᵉ
Tel. +33 (0)1 42 76 09 65 and
55 bis, rue des Saints-Pères, 6ᵉ
Tel. +33 (0)1 42 22 62 58
www.zef.eu

The Jardin du Luxembourg

→ **A favorite park for Left Bank children**—the only problem is there is only a single, narrow strip of grass reserved for picnics. Happily, there's plenty more to do. Here's my ideal itinerary for an afternoon out with the children (and a guaranteed early night afterwards):

❋ **Start at the pond in front of the Senate building.** Hire a little sail-boat to steer with a stick. Watch the ducks.

❋ **Head for the swings** (right next to the tennis courts). Sit them down, and then push!

❋ After an extended swing, **install them in the little pedal cars** on the avenue just behind. Let them pedal to their hearts' content.

❋ Time for a treat after all that effort: a delicious crêpe at the Marionettes snack kiosk!

❋ And on to a show (especially in winter) at the Luxembourg's **indoor puppet theater**. A genuine old-fashioned venue they'll remember for the rest of their lives.

❋ **A quick spin on the merry-go-round** after the theater. There's plenty of opportunity to expend more energy here, too—the man in charge holds out metal hoops for them to catch with a hooked stick.

❋ End the day in fine style with a **pony-ride** (on the avenue opposite the park's Guynemer entrance). And after all that, I guarantee you a quiet evening. Unless *you're* exhausted, too, after such a busy day!

Parc des Buttes Chaumont, 19ᵉ

Often overlooked, because it's off the beaten track, this park has steep hills and deep valleys, with superb views of Paris. Like the Jardin du Luxembourg, there are games, a puppet theater, and pony rides. What do kids like best? The grotto with its stalactites, waterfalls, and suspension footbridge! You can even picnic on the grass. Now that's worth a trip on the metro!

Dressing up

⟶ **Three tips for stylish kids:**

● **Avoid mixing too many loud prints.** Just because they're small doesn't mean you should dress them like clowns.

● **Don't hesitate to dress them in all black.** It's totally dirt-proof, and if you want to brighten things up, add colorful shoes, a scarf, and a bright coat. People over the age of 10 can copy this idea, too!

● **Head off a full-scale fashion rebellion by always letting them choose at least one item in an outfit.** Too bad if your son insists on a fluorescent orange shirt with his favorite super-hero, or your daughter wants to go out in a pink tutu. We've all committed our share of youthful follies.

Bonton

The boutique on rue de Grenelle is delightful and huge, the flagship of the Bonton empire, with everything you could possibly want. The clothes are plain, understated, and very wearable. The secret? A touch of boho style, superb fabrics, and bright (but not too-bright) colors. The look is so successful, it's a shame it stops at children! This new address, just a stone's throw from Merci (see pages 140–143) offers three floors of children's clothes, furniture, and beautiful, funky decorative objects. There's even a children's hair stylist. You can have tea, too, with a selection of pretty, delicious cakes. Children can also take part in creative workshops in-store. The kids' favorite attraction? The vintage black-and-white photo booth (it takes four instant snaps, no digital reworking allowed). There's so much to do you could spend the day here!

5, boulevard des Filles-du-Calvaire, 3ᵉ
Tel. +33 (0)1 42 72 34 69 and
82, rue de Grenelle, 7ᵉ
Tel. +33 (0)1 44 39 09 20
www.bonton.fr

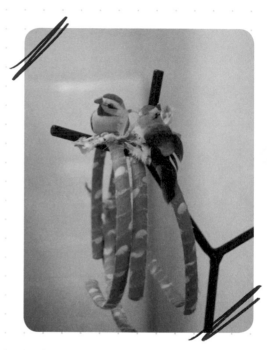

Wowo

The collection is pure Pop, with
a hint of retro, a touch of ethnic
chic, graphic styling, and bright
colors. Fun clothes for fun kids!
Mix them with plain, understated
basics for the perfect look.

5, rue Froissart, 3^e
Tel. +33 (0)1 53 40 84 80
orders: www.alexandalexa.com
www.wowo.fr

www.parisdenfants.com

This website is full of fun ideas
for museum visits or Paris itineraries
(often presented as treasure hunts).
So well planned you'll never
hear your children say "When are
we going home?" or "I can't walk
any more, I want to take the metro!"

Balouga

A fabulous place: *the* children's
furniture pioneer, selling pieces
by leading designers, re-editions of
celebrated vintage classics, and designer
gadgets. A few designer touches in your
children's room will stay lodged in their
memories forever (Balouga's signpost
desk calendar is perfect). Offer them
a touch of French culture—and
prepare Proustian moments for
the years ahead.

25, rue des Filles-du-Calvaire, 3ᵉ
Tel. +33 (0)1 42 74 01 49
www.balouga.com

Agnès b. enfants

The perfect label if you want to dress
your children in black. Agnès b.
was one of the first to boldly go
where grown-up designers had
never dared…. I applaud her style!

Jour Enfant
2, rue du Jour, 1ᵉʳ
Tel. +33 (0)1 40 39 96 88
www.agnesb.com

Musée National d'Histoire Naturelle and the Ménagerie du Jardin des Plantes

Every Parisian child has been here at least once (often on a school outing) to admire the fabulous Grand Gallery of Evolution, a Noah's Ark parade of taxidermic animals. When the sun shines, head for the zoo, one of the oldest in Europe. Trying to pry your children away from the monkey enclosure when the zoo is about to close is one of the great experiences of Parisian parenthood! What's new at the garden? Four amazing tropical greenhouses, recently reopened after a five-year renovation project.

36, rue Geoffroy Saint-Hilaire, 5ᵉ
Tel. 01 40 79 54 79
www.mnhn.fr

Tour Montparnasse

The best view of Paris: you can see the Eiffel Tower, but not the Tour Montparnasse itself!

33, avenue du Maine, 15ᵉ
Tel. +33 (0)1 45 38 52 56
www.tourmontparnasse56.com

The cafe at the musée Rodin

A great place for lunch with the children in summer: the museum's park is a haven of greenery, full of world-famous statues. Culture and fresh air all at once—the ultimate Parisian children's outing!

79, rue de Varenne, 7ᵉ
Tel. +33 (0)1 44 18 61 10
www.musee-rodin.fr

Musée Carnavalet

The two mansions housing the museum are worth a visit in their own right, but this museum is a great way to introduce children to the history of Paris. Did you know a mammoth's tooth was found under the Avenue Dausmesnil in the 12e? You'll find out about that and much more here. The children will still be talking about their visit days later. The museum houses some 600,000 works—you'll be back!

23, rue de Sévigné, 3e
Tel. 01 44 59 58 31
www.carnavalet.paris.fr

Shakespeare & Company

Climb the stairs at the back of this legendary Paris institution, to the cozy children's section stocked with English and American favorites, comfy cushions, even the resident cat!

37, rue de la Bûcherie, 5e
Tel: +33 (0)1 43 25 40 93
www.shakespeareandcompany.com

Jardin des Tuileries, 1er

If your kids love bouncing on the beds when they have nothing to do, take them to the Tuileries, where eight large trampolines stand ready for take-off. A lot more fun than sitting on a merry-go-round! There are merry-go-rounds, too, for more sedate entertainment.

Eiffel Tower

Unmissable! Beat the crowds—buy your tickets in advance, online at www.tour-eiffel.fr.
Or for the family with stamina: walk up the steps.

Pain d'épices

A unique place in a typically Parisian covered arcade. This traditional toyshop is dollhouse heaven: there are houses of all sizes, and everything you need to furnish one, even the toilet! Not forgetting tiny cakes for the kitchen, or a mini Monopoly set. For a personalized present, I buy one of the glass-fronted presentation boxes and fill them with objects that say something about the recipient—an electric drill for a DIY fan, a doll's dress for a fashionista.

Librairie Chantelivre

A temple to children's books. The window displays are full of great ideas. This bookshop makes children *want* to read French—bravo!

13, rue de Sèvres, 6ᵉ
Tel. +33 (0)1 45 48 87 90
www.chantelivre.fr

29–31, passage Jouffroy, 9ᵉ
Tel. +33 (0)1 47 70 08 68
www.paindepices.fr

Jardin Catherine Labouré

→ **29 rue de Babylone, 7ᵉ**

Hidden behind walls, it's invisible from the street, but this is one of Paris's very few parks where walking on the grass is allowed. For a chic picnic, stock up at the Grande Epicerie, nearby. A park for those in the know—you'll never stumble across it by accident!

Luco

The ultimate Left Bank venue: "Luco" is a Parisian children's nickname for the area around the Jardin de Luxembourg. The clothes are plain and understated, elegant, but with a touch of rock'n'roll. The essence of Parisian chic!

24, rue de Babylone, 7ᵉ
Tel. +33 (0)1 42 84 35 47
www.luco.fr

Palais de Tokyo and Tokyo Eat

This museum of contemporary art doesn't have a permanent collection, but a changing program of interesting temporary exhibitions. Children come here for the creative workshops—*Les Ateliers Tok-Tok*. Budding artists are taken on a tour of the current show, and create their own work of art inspired by what they have seen. Arty types even host their birthday parties here ("Mon Annivarty"). Next stop, the ultra-designer restaurant, with a delicious children's menu including great burgers. Adults love the contemporary-chic menu, too. Sunday booking strongly recommended.

13, avenue du Président Wilson, 16ᵉ
Palais de Tokyo: Tel. +33 (0)1 47 23 54 01
Restaurant Tokyo Eat:
Tel. +33 (0)1 47 20 00 29
www.palaisdetokyo.com

6 e-boutiques to click with the kids

www.ovale.com
For luxury new-born gifts, like the solid silver rattle (it turns into a key-ring when baby grows up). London: 35b, Sloane Street +44 (0)207 2355235

www.aliceaparis.com
Natural fabrics, simple shapes, affordable prices—the perfect trio!

www.talcboutique.com
Minimalism and creativity in one label—a fashion feat for this brand aimed at children aged 3 months to 10 years. There are a couple of "real" boutiques in Paris, too (60, rue Saintonge, 3ᵉ and 7, rue des Quatre-Vents, 6ᵉ).

www.littlefashiongallery.com
An indispensable e-address for anyone looking for trendy but sharp children's clothes. And click here for ages 10–20: www.mediumfashiongallery.com.

www.smallable.com
A site dedicated to small, wonderfully hip labels and eco-friendly designer toys.

www.petitstock.com
Top labels at rock-bottom prices. Parisians love it!

Serendipity

For parents looking for unusual ways to decorate their children's bedrooms. This boutique can be summed up in just one word: eclectic. If you're looking for cardboard cradles, or a traditional school desk and bench, here they are. A star-spangled bedspread? No problem! Untreated wood, hand-crafted furniture, natural fabrics and materials—totally twenty-first century!

81–83, rue du Cherche-Midi, 6ᵉ
Tel. + 33 (0)1 40 46 01 15
www.serendipity.fr

École Ritz-Escoffier

What do you give a child who wants to be Rémy the Rat from *Ratatouille*? A cooking class at the Ritz-Escoffier school, of course, in the kitchens of the Paris Ritz itself! Budding chefs don full kitchen whites and learn how to prepare dishes selected from the school's website. Everyone takes their creations home to enjoy afterwards—and they're sure to ask for more!

15, place Vendôme, 1ᵉʳ
student entrance: 38, rue Cambon, 1ᵉʳ
Tel. +33 (0)1 43 16 16 30
www.ritzparis.com

Ie

A pretty place selling delightful fabrics by the meter, together with other delectable treasures guaranteed to stimulate your creative imagination! The stationery section is a treat, with an array of small, vintage-style notebooks. Ie also sells children's clothes made in India using natural fabrics, woven and printed by hand. Sustainable fashion!

128, rue Vieille-du-Temple, 3ᵉ
Tel. + 33 (0)1 44 59 87 72

3. Parisian Wellness

Every Parisian knows that looking and feeling your best go hand in hand. Here are the Parisian addresses that hold the keys to being your very best.

Françoise Morice

The ultimate professional salon. Françoise is skilled in the art of transforming your complexion and removing signs of fatigue. She has also developed a unique technique—kineplasty—designed to rejuvenate, tone, and smooth away lines. It really works! I left the salon promising myself I would come back every week. (I haven't had time, *bien sûr!*)

58 bis, rue François 1er, 8e
Tel. +33 (0)1 42 56 14 08
www.francoise-morice.fr

Six Senses

This brand-new spa boasts supernatural decor—treatment cabins shaped like wooden cocoons, and a "green wall" of live vegetation in the reception area. The venue is part of the worldwide Six Senses group, but Parisians adore its homegrown facial using Parisian rooftop honey. Bees born and raised in the nearby Tuileries gardens produce the spa's own honey in rooftop hives. How very Parisian!

3, rue de Castiglione, 1er
Tel. +33 (0)1 43 16 10 10
www.sixsenses.com

Nuxe

Every Parisian uses at least one Nuxe product (Huile Prodigieuse is a must), bought in the pharmacy or supermarket. (French women love buying supermarket toiletries and beauty products!) And the new Nuxe spa is heaven! The decor—in natural colors, with exposed stonework—sets a Zen-like atmosphere from the reception area on in.

32, rue Montorgueil, 1er
Tel. +33 (0)1 42 36 65 65
www.nuxe.com

Hair

Studio 34

A warm, super-welcoming salon nested in a courtyard full of plants. Delphine Courteille is a hair designer and regular backstage at Paris's top runway shows. Her salon looks more like a private apartment, frequented by a host of celebrity clients. For colors, ask for Jean, a longtime colleague of Christophe Robin (who sweetly agreed to turn me blond when no one else dared).

34, rue du Mont-Thabor, 1er
Tel. +33 (0)1 47 03 35 35
www.delphinecourteille.com

Très confidentiel Bernard Friboulet

In a pure white, laboratory-style setting, stylist Bernard Friboulet—a true artist who often officiates at photography shoots—dispenses Shu Uemura Art of Hair, a fabulous collection of treatments conceived as veritable rituals along the lines of a Japanese tea ceremony. Try them soon! Best of all, Bernard asks plenty of questions before taking up his scissors—a guarantee there will be no unpleasant surprises.

Jardins du Palais Royal
44–45, galerie de Montpensier, 1er
Tel +33 (0)1 97 43 98

Romain Colors

The address for ultra-natural color. Romain uses vegetable colors with an extremely subtle approach. He knows exactly how to give dark hair that essential gloss, and is highly skilled in the fine art of perfect blond streaks. Best of all, his fine highlights are always carefully worked to avoid visible roots once your hair has grown in. The salon, like its owner, is friendly and welcoming. The salon's stylists deliver expert cuts and (amazingly) never take off more than you wish! More good news—the salon is open very late on Wednesdays. Book now!

37, rue Rousselet, 7ᵉ
Tel. +33 (0)1 42 73 24 19
www.romaincolors.fr

Express manicure.

Manucurist Refresh

Every Parisian knows how to do her own expert manicure at home, but occasionally she calls on the professionals— no appointment necessary— at Manucurist Refresh.

4, rue de Castellane, 8ᵉ
Tel. +33 (0)1 42 65 19 30 and
13, rue Chaussée d'Antin, 9ᵉ
Tel. + 33 (0)1 47 03 37 33
www.manucurist.com

Les Salons du Palais Royal/ Les parfums de Serge Lutens

A sublime setting. Serge Lutens fragrances are full of personality. My own favorite is Amber Sultan— a wonderfully spicy perfume for summer. This is a great place to shop for gifts—the magnificent bottles can be engraved with the recipient's initials. Don't miss their adorable red lipstick, in a special mini format, perfect for keeping in your bag.

Jardin du Palais Royal
142, rue de Valois, 1er
Tel. +33 (0)1 49 27 09 09
www.salons-shiseido.com

Guerlain

Legendary! Guerlain is the iconic home of luxury perfumes "Made in France." Monsieur Guerlain still presides, coming up with new fragrance ideas. The cult house perfumes (Mitsouko, Shalimar, Habit Rouge, Vétiver) complement the Parisian collection, featuring new editions of landmark fragrances from the history of Guerlain. Don't forget their celebrated Terracotta powder, delivering a healthy complexion to office-bound Parisians who seldom see the sun.

68, avenue des Champs-Élysées, 8e
Tel. +33 (0)1 45 62 52 57
www.guerlain.com

Maison Francis Kurkdjian

A handsome place to find scented gifts: the eaux de cologne baptised simply "for day" (*pour le matin*) and "for evening" (*pour le soir*) are heavenly. For fun (and to amuse the kids) you can blow pear-scented soap bubbles. The ultimate in chic? Scented laundry soap that makes you want to wash your sweaters every day.

5, rue d'Alger, 1er
Tel. +33 (0)1 42 60 07 07
www.franciskurkdjian.com

Éditions de Parfums/ Frédéric Malle

Parisians love these original creations concocted by the perfume world's top "nose." True works of olfactory art! The room fragrances are irresistible.

37, rue de Grenelle, 7e
Tel. +33 (0)1 42 22 76 40
www.editionsdeparfums.com

Diptyque

Parisians adore the scented candles, but Diptyque makes intoxicating fragrances, too, including the woody, sophisticated scent, Philosykos. Their beauty-products are also a must, including the utterly fabulous Lait Frais, scented with orange flower.

34, boulevard Saint-Germain, 5e
Tel. +33 (0)1 01 43 26 77 44
www.diptyqueparis.com

The best candles

Cire Trudon

The world's oldest candle maker,
is carefully watched after by the
talented artistic director Ramdane
Touhami. A Trudon is the equivalent
of a Hermès handbag, but in the
form of a candle. Give your friend
L'admirable, with its irresistible eaux
de cologne scent. And tell her "an
It candle is even more mystical than
an It bag!"

New York: 54 Bond Street
Paris: 78 rue de Seine, 6ᵉ
Tel. + 33 (0)1 43 26 46 50
www.ciretrudon.com

Paris's top five florists

ARÔM PARIS

Wonderfully creative bouquets. Often called in to create designs for ultra-fashionable soirées.

196, rue du Faubourg Saint-Antoine, 12ᵉ
Tel. + 33 (0)1 40 09 91 38
www.aromparis.fr

ODORANTES

Ultra-modern. Everyone loves the black packaging, adding instant depth to the freshest, simplest bouquet.

9, rue Madame, 6ᵉ
Tel. + 33 (0)1 42 84 03 00
www.odorantes-paris.com

LACHAUME

Sophisticated, haute-couture creations.

10, rue Royale, 8ᵉ
Tel. + 33 (0)1 42 60 59 74
www.lachaume-fleurs.com

MOULIÉ

In the great French tradition. Moulié is known as the supplier of government officals, embassies, and top couturiers.

8, place du Palais-Bourbon, 7ᵉ
Tel. + 33 (0)1 45 51 78 43
www.mouliefleurs.com

ROSES COSTES DANI ROSES

Sublime roses and special creations by Dani, a true Parisian and a venerable artist.

239, rue Saint-Honoré, 1ᵉʳ
Tel. + 33 (0)1 42 44 50 09

4. Bon Appetit!

Paris is world-renowned for its gastronomic delights, from the simple baguette to the finest grand cru. From the classic bistro to the Michelin-starred temple of haute cuisine, the City of Lights offers something for everyone. Rows of cafés line the streets and their terraces serve as the perfect rendezvous point for a morning coffee or an evening aperitif. Here are my favorite spots in the city.

Classic restaurants

Look no further for the essence of Paris! The Parisian will often order-in sushi (just like in *Sex and the City*) but the city's bistros and restaurants are her favorite venues for gossiping with the girls.

Le Café de Flore

The essential Flore

So synonymous with Paris it's virtually a cliché, yet the Flore is also the beating heart of Saint-Germain-des-Prés, a state of mind in its own right, evocative of Existentialist thinkers such as Jean-Paul Sartre and Simone de Beauvoir, and of Françoise Sagan, Boris Vian, Miles Davis. Above all it's the quintessence of the French spirit: rebellious, provocative, generous, non-conformist. Often a gathering-place for the Left (like the Bank on which it stands).

The paradoxical Flore

✱ You can find a quiet corner (especially on the second floor) BUT you're guaranteed to run into a horde of people you know.

✱ It's a highly contemporary place BUT the decor is old-fashioned.

✱ It's a restaurant BUT you can stop in for a coffee.

✱ It's friendly and intimate BUT huge.

✱ It's unconventional BUT an institution.

✱ You may come across writer and politician Jorge Semprun, directors Steven Spielberg and Sofia Coppola, or lawyer and ex-minister Georges Kiejman BUT there's a host of fashion folk, too … and me!

IN A NUTSHELL

Were you at the reception
for the last Prix de Flore?
Oh, you weren't invited?
What a shame!

Where to sit?

🖊 Left of the entrance, near
the cash register is the regulars' spot.
Upstairs, if you want some peace
and quiet and a little more light.
But wherever you choose, the lady
at the cash register will keep a
friendly eye out, and the waiters will
serve you politely, with a touch of wit.
A great atmosphere fostered by owner
Miroslav Siljegovic.

When to go?

🖊 On the weekend, for lunch.
But it's also the ideal meeting-point
when you have no idea how
many are coming. For lunch with
a girlfriend. At night for a dinner
with a lover, or with friends. You
can spend a lifetime at the Flore.

What to order?

✳ The Colette salad
(with grapefruit, lettuce hearts,
and avocado).

✳ Lightly cooked scrambled egg.

✳ Welsh Rarebit (toast topped
with a mixture of melted cheese,
mustard, and beer). Very filling,
and delicious.

✳ Le Flore (the house
croque-monsieur).

✳ The green bean salad (a little
basic, perhaps, but the beans
are cooked *al dente*, to perfection).

✳ Hot chocolate with a cloud of
Chantilly cream, or a *chocolat liégeois*.

Dress code

⟶ Relaxed Left Bank chic
(jeans, a blazer, ballet flats).
A word of advice: avoid red (the
color of the banquette seating) or
you may go completely unnoticed.

172, boulevard Saint-Germain, 6ᵉ
Tel. +33 (0)1 45 48 55 26
Open daily, 7 a.m. to 2 a.m.
www.cafedeflore.fr

Chartreux

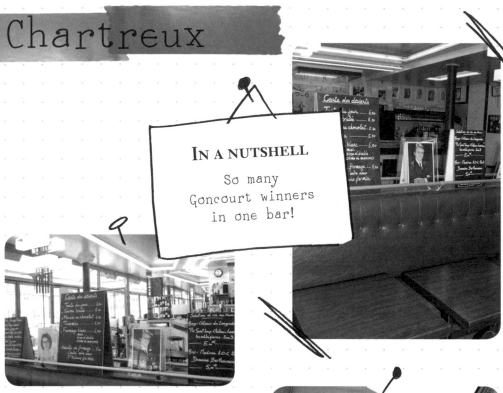

IN A NUTSHELL

So many
Goncourt winners
in one bar!

Worth knowing

🖌 The official HQ of parents from the neighboring school, so it is packed for coffee every morning around 8:30 a.m. Similarly packed with students at lunchtime. A favorite neighborhood spot at night.

Decor

🖌 Moleskin banquettes, formica tables, totally Parisian roots. Everyone adores the photos of artists on the wall and the untouched original features.

What to order

✱ Dishes of the day (whatever they are), burgers, fruit tarts.

8, rue des Chartreux, 6ᵉ
Tel. +33 (0)1 43 26 66 34

Chez Paul

Worth knowing

On the very cute place Dauphine, an archetypal restaurant with theatrical decor.

Decor

Retro classic, of course. A vaulted cellar and exposed stonework—the quintessential old-world Paris bistro.

What to order

Duck *aiguillettes* in a light sweet-and-sour sauce.

15, place Dauphine, 1ᵉʳ
Tel. +33 (0)8 99 69 05 81

La Closerie des Lilas

IN A NUTSHELL

Hemingway came here when he was writing *The Sun also Rises*. I bet he ordered the caramelized pork ribs with honey!

Worth knowing

🍴 The formal restaurant is ultra-chic; the brasserie is much more affordable. I head for the latter, after asking the *écailler* out front for his tips on the day's seafood.

Decor

🍴 Padded leather banquettes, dark wooden tables, place mats signed by passing celebs. Genuine "cozy Parisian."

What to order

✳ The steak tartare—the house "must." Everything else is delicious, too!

171, boulevard du Montparnasse, 6ᵉ
Tel. + 33 (0)1 40 51 34 50

La Fontaine de Mars

IN A NUTSHELL

i'll have what Michelle Obama had when she came here!

Worth knowing

Everyone comes here when the sun shines to take advantage of the terrace.

Decor

Red-and-white gingham tablecloths, floor tiles from the year 1900, and a waiter in a white apron of the same vintage. Pure Paris!

What to order

A different dish of the day, every weekday. On Fridays, try the roast farm chicken and mashed potatoes. The *à la carte* menu has delicious snails and a fine duck *magret*.

129, rue Saint-Dominique, 7ᵉ
Tel. +33 (0)1 74 05 46 44
www.fontainedemars.com

Cafés de l'Industrie

World knowing

🥄 There are three Cafés de l'Industrie spread over three addresses on both sides of the street. The one to visit is no. 16 (the biggest).

Decor

🥄 Old colonial with lots of dark wood, ocher walls, black-and-white photos, and a really great atmosphere, especially at night. The perfect spot to soak-up true Parisian style.

What to order

✗ Salads, carpaccio, traditional French dishes, and plenty of other good things chalked-up on the board.

16, rue Saint-Sabin, 11ᵉ
Tel. + 33 (0)1 47 00 13 53

IN A NUTSHELL

Wow, you can
stay 'til 2 a.m.!

Racines

IN A NUTSHELL

What a fabulous bistronomique!*

*The perhaps unfamiliar term *bistronomique* is used to describe a new-style bistro that offers creative cuisine worthy of gourmet restaurants, but at a reasonable price.

Worth knowing

This is a very small place, the regulars don't like making room, and the owner refuses to serve more than thirty tables a day, so booking is absolutely essential.

Decor

Closely packed bistro tables, bottles of wine (for sale) lining the walls. Racines is a mini eaterie in a pretty Belle Epoque arcade, the Passage des Panoramas. The heart and soul of Paris.

What to order

The specials on the blackboard change daily, and the produce is superb. My favorite? Fattened hen with spring vegetables. And remember: this is a temple of fine wine, too.

8, passage des Panoramas, 2ᵉ
Tel. +33 (0)1 40 13 06 41

Au bon Saint-Pourçain

Worth knowing

Unassuming to look at, but located on a charming, typically Parisian street near the church of Saint-Sulpice.

Decor

Red-and-white checked tablecloths outside, white lace curtains inside. Set this restaurant down anywhere on Earth, and people will say: "It's French!"

What to order

This place does just what it says out front: *cuisine bourgeoise*—leeks vinaigrette, duck terrine, knuckle of lamb, chicken with mushrooms, etc. Not to mention their famous *tête de veau gribiche* (jellied veal with egg mayonnaise and capers). And a bottle of Saint-Pourçain, of course!

10 bis, rue Servandoni, 6ᵉ
Tel. +33 (0)1 43 54 93 63

Le Café de l'Odéon

IN A NUTSHELL
It's like being in a play!

Worth knowing

Make the most of the lovely terrace as soon as spring comes: on place de l'Odéon, just in front of the Théâtre de l'Odéon. You can have dinner outside, too.

Decor

Theatrical with marble columns, grandiose chandeliers, gilded mirrors, and antique statues. Much more sober on the terrace, but with the Paris sky overhead!

What to order

Fillet of beef.

Place du Théâtre de l'Odéon, 6ᵉ
Tel. +33 (0)1 44 85 41 30
www.cafedelodeon.com

L'Écume Saint-Honoré

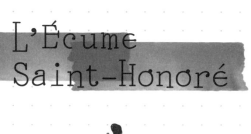

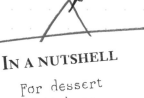

IN A NUTSHELL

For dessert i'll have a scallop!

Worth knowing

It all started with a fishmonger's shop, then an oyster bar….

Decor

Maritime, with a sky-blue ceiling painted with clouds and seagulls. Seagull cries on the soundtrack.

What to order

Let's be clear, this is not the place for steak. It's seafood and shellfish all the way.

6, rue du Marché-Saint-Honoré, 1er
Tel. +33 (0)1 42 61 93 87

Chez Georges

IN A NUTSHELL

There's another place called Georges at the top of the Centre Pompidou. It's not bad; you can see all of Paris from your table. Here, you can see *le tout Paris*, without even looking out of the window!

Worth knowing

Nothing changes here, least of all the menu. *Andouillettes* (tripe sausage), celery *rémoulade*, herrings in oil with potatoes and apple, profiteroles. Everything is always available, hurrah.

Decor

Belle Epoque bistro, unchanged through the decades. A genuine, appealing atmosphere of old Parisian chic.

What to order

The classic *pavé du Mail*, a perfect cut of beef with fries.

1, rue du Mail, 2e
Tel. +33 (0)1 42 60 07 11

Le Salon du Cinéma du Panthéon

Worth knowing

On the first floor of one of Paris's oldest cinemas. Ideal for lunch with your girlfriends, or afternoon tea (it closes at 7 p.m.).

Decor

The 1,600-square-foot-space has been decorated by Catherine Deneuve herself, with star designer Christian Sapet. Big cozy sofas, coffee tables, and statement lamps make for a relaxed, comfy atmosphere you won't want to leave.

What to order

Succulent salads, Spanish charcuterie, organic salmon. All fresh and delicious.

13, rue Victor Cousin, 6ᵉ
Tel. + 33 (0)1 56 24 88 80

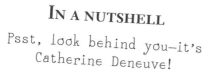

IN A NUTSHELL

Psst, look behind you—it's
Catherine Deneuve!

Hot
Spots

Paris has its hot new addresses, attracting the
It crowd, too. Booking is absolutely essential,
and some places even have waiting lists.
(Just like the latest It bag....)

High fashion

La Société

Opposite the church of Saint-Germain, hidden behind a huge coach door, the Société (a Costes restaurant) can seem intimidating. (And rumor has it the owner doesn't like to be featured in guidebooks.) Decorated by interior designer Christian Liaigre, the ultra-modern setting is as minimalist and understated as the food. Try the *tartare aller-retour* for instant branding as a super-fashionable Parisian!

4, place Saint-Germain, 6ᵉ
Tel. +33 (0)1 53 63 60 60

Carnivore heaven

Unico

In the heart of the 11ᵉ arrondissement, this Argentinian restaurant is always buzzing. Unsurprisingly, given that the (Argentinian) owners have hit on the perfect formula. The restaurant is installed in a 1970s butcher's shop, with the original decor intact (i.e. *very* orange), serving beef imported direct from the Pampas—full of flavor and meltingly tender. There is also an unmissable *banana con dulce de leche*. Not a place for dieters, but you'll roar with pleasure!

15, rue Paul Bert, 11ᵉ
Tel. +33 (0)1 43 67 68 08
www.resto-unico.com

Cuisine très nouvelle

Le Chateaubriand

There is no such thing as a Parisian who hasn't been to the Chateaubriand! Of course, everyone swoons for the fiery Basque chef Inaki Aizpitarte, but they love his highly inventive cooking, too. (Who wouldn't?) Inaki's offbeat experiments have included sardines in their own foie gras, or raw cep mushrooms in coffee oil. Fabulously good. His bold mixes are the essence of *nouvelle Paris cuisine*. The bistro's raw decor is a great success, too, and offers a feast for the eyes as well!

129, avenue Parmentier, 11ᵉ
Tel. +33 (0)1 43 57 45 95

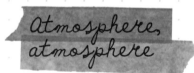

Atmosphere, atmosphere

Le Baratin

It's been open a while, but the fabulous atmosphere remains unchanged. The team is wonderfully friendly, and the food's great too. I remember an amazing tuna tartare with cherry. And the exotic beef strips are worth the trek to the 20ᵉ arrondissement. Simple and good. So go!

3, rue Jouye-Rouve, 20ᵉ
Tel. +33 (0)1 43 49 39 70

Overlooking the Eiffel Tower

Le Café de l'Homme

The official best view of the Eiffel Tower. In summer the Café de l'Homme's stunning terrace is the place for dinner with visiting friends from out of town, or *en tête-à-tête* for a marriage proposal. The contemporary cuisine is truly delicious: try the pan-fried *escalope* of foie gras with a Granny Smith emulsion, the plancha-grilled lacquered tuna with soy, or the cheesecake with *fromage blanc* ice cream. My mouth's watering already!

17, place du Trocadéro, 16ᵉ
Tel. +33 (0)1 44 05 30 15
www.restaurant-cafedelhomme.com

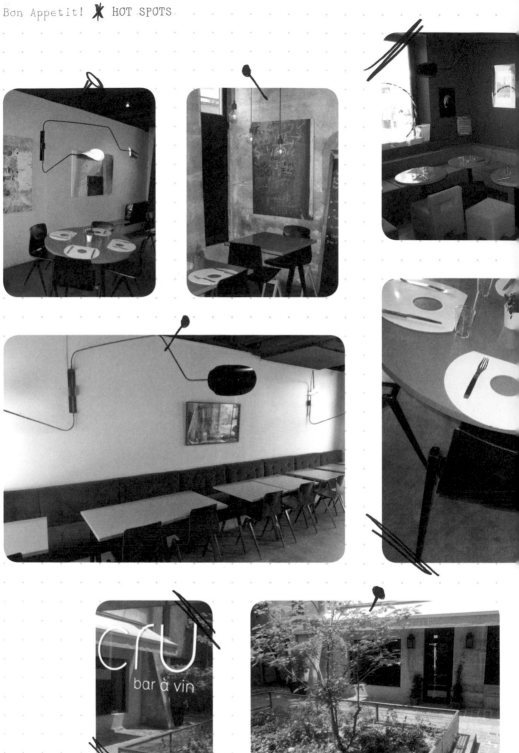

cru
bar à vin

Contemporary chic

Cru

As the name implies, this is a temple to raw food (the triple tartare platter is divine!) and wonderful carpaccios, although they also serve cooked dishes like duck *magret* with honey and sesame seeds (the mouth waters just talking about it). Exquisite! Just like the owner Marie Steinberg. Everything is in impeccable taste, beginning with the designer decor. (Check out the toilets, they're great fun!) The small courtyard is delightful in summer and service is friendly. I could happily lunch here every day and come back on Sunday for brunch with my children. A fine Cru!

7, rue Charlemagne, 4ᵉ
Tel. +33 (0)1 40 27 81 84
www.restaurantcru.fr

Go Gourmet

The Parisian may be a petite size 2
(rest assured, I do know a few size 4s…)
but she's unlikely to skip lunch
and shop till she drops. Always know
when to sit down and savor a tasty salad!

Bread & Roses

Bread & Roses have an existing outlet in the 6ᵉ arrondissement (7, rue de Fleurus), so I was thrilled when their new branch opened early in 2010 near my office. Now it's my official cafeteria. Their quiches, savory tomato and buffalo mozzarella tarts, and salads are excellent, and their organic wholegrain bread will have you coming back for more. Not to mention the pastries (Mont-Blanc chocolate mousse cakes, cheesecakes, millefeuilles). For organic bread to nibble back at the office, visit the bakery counter at the back of the restaurant.

Emporio Armani Caffè

Above the Armani boutique. Ultra-chic, like the label. Excellent, sophisticated Italian cuisine, and the best *vitello tonnato* in all of Paris.

25, rue Boissy d'Anglas, 8ᵉ
Tel. +33 (0)1 47 42 40 00
www.breadandroses.fr

149, boulevard Saint-Germain, 6ᵉ
Tel. +33 (0)1 45 48 62 15

jour

The high temple of made-to-measure salads. Compose your own from six bases, forty-two toppings, and eight sauces—a different combination for every day of the year. Check the locations on the Internet before stepping out for your Paris shopping spree—they have ten branches across the city.

13, boulevard de Malesherbes, 8ᵉ
Tel. +33 (0)1 40 07 06 68
www.jour.fr

Ralph's

Ralph Lauren rightly chose the Left Bank for his biggest European flagship store. The restored seventeenth-century townhouse is dedicated to the creations of the king of US sportswear. The icing on the cake is Ralph's restaurant, in a leafy inner courtyard. In the heart of Paris, the menu is all-American (crab cakes and burgers). The Parisian loves a change of scene!

173, boulevard Saint-Germain, 6ᵉ
Tel. +33 (0)1 44 77 76 00
www.ralphlauren.com

Cojean

Healthy sandwiches do exist! Cojean is a fast-food outlet that's good for you, serving fabulous mini sandwiches and brioches. The soups are 100% vegetarian, the quiches are ultra-fresh, and the freshly pressed juices and fruit smoothies are a treat!

6, rue de Sèze, 9ᵉ
Tel. +33 (0)1 40 06 08 80
www.cojean.fr

Rose Bakery

Hard to find if you don't know it already, but well worth the effort. The Rose is a grocery store, lunchtime restaurant, and tearoom, with a "back-to-nature" atmosphere and the emphasis on super-fresh, organic food. For cakes, fruit juice, salads. It's good to treat yourself!

30, rue Debelleyme, 3ᵉ
Tel. +33 (0)1 49 96 54 01

Le Water-Bar de Colette

The Colette boutique is on every Parisian's orbit. Check the store for all the latest trends, then head to the basement for lunch—a feast of "fashion-food" including vegetarian lasagna and desserts by a host of high-profile chefs. All washed down with the latest "designer" waters. A hip legend in its own lunchtime!

213, rue Saint-Honoré, 1ᵉʳ
Tel. +33 (0)1 55 35 33 90
www.colette.fr

5. Bonne Nuit !

Where to sleep in Paris? The city's legendary palace hotels are one solution— guests are rarely disappointed by the Ritz or the Plaza Athénée. But there's a vast choice of attractive small hotels, too. Here's my selection of the best places to stay— wonderful locations, pleasant service, attractive decor, and an extra dose of charm.

Rustic charm

Hôtel des Grandes Écoles

IN A NUTSHELL

There's no TV—all the better to hear the birds singing in the courtyard!

THE DECOR

✳ Flowery wallpaper, crocheted bedspreads, and exposed woodwork: twenty-first-century designer chic is a world away.

75, rue Cardinal-Lemoine, 5e
Tel. +33 (0)1 43 26 79 23
From 115€
www.hotel-grandes-ecoles.com

THE ATMOSPHERE

✳ In the heart of the 5e arrondissement, this hotel is a real touch of French rustic charm. It looks like a country retreat, wonderfully quiet and surrounded by greenery. In summer, breakfast is served on the grounds, under the trees. An address for people who want to experience Paris but sleep in the country.

Classic charm

Hôtel de l'Abbaye Saint-Germain

IN A NUTSHELL
It's soooo charming!

THE DECOR

✳ Floral or striped wallpaper, huge giltwood mirrors, headboards to match the lampshades, and marble bathrooms: 100% classic grand style.

THE ATMOSPHERE

✳ Very peaceful. This is one of Paris's refined, classic, affordable hotels in Saint-Germain-des-Prés. It's a great favorite with fashionistas (you can drop off your shopping bags in just a few minutes). In summer, breakfast is served in the leafy courtyard, to the splashing of the fountain—one of the hotel's many attractions!

10, rue Cassette, 6ᵉ
Tel. +33 (0)1 45 44 38 11
From 260€ (240€ if you book online)
www.hotelabbayeparis.com

Pure Left Bank

L'Hôtel

IN A NUTSHELL

Oscar Wilde liked it here; you'll love it!

THE DECOR

✳ By Jacques Garcia, so there is lots of red velvet, antiques, gilt standard lamps and fringed shades, patterned wallpaper, and rich fabrics—a cozy, classic look. The terrace adjoining the largest suite, overlooking the rooftops of Paris, is simply fabulous.

THE ATMOSPHERE

✳ There's a sense of history as soon as you step inside. The hotel was once part of the Paris residence of France's notorious Queen Margot. After its recent makeover, it has become a fashion-world favorite. Don't miss the new restaurant (aptly named "Le Restaurant") and the vaulted pool in the cellar, for guests only.

13, rue des Beaux-Arts, 6^e
Tel. +33 (0)1 44 41 99 00
From 255€
www.l-hotel.com

The allure of Montmartre

Hôtel Particulier

IN A NUTSHELL

Shall we have cocktails in the garden, or play Amélie Poulain in the Café des 2 Moulins? (nearby at 15, rue Lepic, in the 18ᵉ).

THE ATMOSPHERE

I prefer the Left Bank, but I have a soft spot for Montmartre. In the secret passage known as the Rocher de la Sorcière ("the Witch's Rock"!), this grand Directoire townhouse is sure to delight visiting fashionistas. Five suites all overlook the delightful garden (it's also wonderfully quiet, of course).

23, avenue Junot, Pavillon D, 18ᵉ
From 290€. Special rates at certain times of year.
www.hotel-particulier-montmartre.com

THE DECOR

Conceived as a private house with each bedroom individually decorated, designer Morgane Rousseau has called in a host of artists to help with the interior. The result is eclectic, contemporary, and very *à la mode*. A black bath takes pride of place in the "Loft" suite, print wallpaper takes you straight out into the garden in the "Végétale" suite, while the "Poèmes et Chapeaux" suite boasts a black bowler-hat lamp-shade and white walls.

Home away from home

Hôtel
Recamier

THE ATMOSPHERE

✳ This hotel (an old, trusted
favorite of mine) was renovated in
2009 in the style of a delightful private
house: the result is discreet luxury
with a hint of the 1940s. This is the
hot new address whispered by word
of mouth around Paris. Wonderfully
located next to the church of Saint-
Sulpice, with a genuinely warm,
friendly welcome.

THE DECOR

✳ Each floor has its own color
scheme, and each bedroom is
different—a finely striped woolen
carpet and wall coverings in natural
fibers in one (my favorite); a checkered
headboard and cross-patterned fabrics
in another. There are Fragonard
toiletries in the bathrooms, too,
making the hotel worth a visit for that
reason alone!

3 bis, place Saint-Sulpice, 6ᵉ
Tel. +33 (0)1 43 26 04 89
From 250€
www.hotelrecamier.com

Relaxed chic, with children

Hôtel Bel Ami

IN A NUTSHELL

The children don't want to go out, they just want to stay in the hotel!

THE ATMOSPHERE

✳ Design, design, and more design, but with a friendly, relaxed touch. Especially when it comes to children, who can sleep next door in a connecting bedroom, specially prepared with Teddy bears, coloring books, and crayons. There's a junior menu and (for older children) a selection of computer games—kids are valued clients, too! The hotel's regular jazz concerts are very popular, attracting a crowd of locals. And the same goes for the spa.

THE DECOR

✳ Casual chic. Solid oak furniture, natural colors with touches of dark brown and black. Lacquered bathrooms. Each bedroom has its own key color: cinnamon, cumin, aniseed, or orange.

7–11, rue Saint-Benoît, 6ᵉ
Tel. +33 (0)1 42 61 53 53
From 250€
www.hotelbelami.fr

Back to the Belle Epoque
Le Régina

IN A NUTSHELL

People never think of coming here for a drink, so it's a great place for a lovers' tryst, with no fear of being spotted!

THE ATMOSPHERE

✳ One of Paris's best-preserved Belle Epoque palace hotels. It's popular with tourists, but a few Parisians in the know love the discreet, intimate Bar Anglais, or the restaurant with a small terrace in a leafy courtyard.

2, place des Pyramides, 1er
Tel. +33 (0)1 42 60 31 10
From 375€
www.regina-hotel.com

THE DECOR

✳ Everything looks as if it's been here since the hotel opened in 1900. Foreign visitors arriving here, just a stone's throw from the Louvre, feel as if they've truly discovered a corner of Old Paree. Red velvet armchairs, marble tiles, chandeliers, and tented bed hangings give an air of old-world charm. A world away from the contemporary designer chic of the Colette boutique, nearby!

Discreet Luxury

Hôtel Villa Madame

IN A NUTSHELL

So chic and cozy, all at once!

THE ATMOSPHERE

✱ Unpretentious luxury: a discreet address offering contemporary chic in a charming street in the 6ᵉ arrondissement, with a small garden as a bonus!

THE DECOR

✱ Pale wood, exotic decorative objects, and a color scheme of beige, brown, white, and delicate orchid shades set the tone for this designer hotel with a warm, welcoming touch. Ask for the bedrooms with terraces, for the views over the rooftops of Paris.

44, rue Madame, 6ᵉ
Tel. +33 (0)1 45 48 02 81
From 192€
www.hotelvillamadameparis.com

HOTELS FOR ALL REASONS:

For a lovers' tryst

L'Hôtel Amour
8, rue Navarin, 9ᵉ
Tel. +33 (0)1 48 78 31 80
Double rooms from 150€.
www.hotelamourparis.fr

To wake up on the Place des Vosges

Le Pavillon de la Reine
28, place des Vosges, 3ᵉ
Tel. +33 (0)1 40 29 19 19
From 330€
www.pavillon-de-la-reine.com

On a budget

Hôtel Sainte-Beuve
9, rue Sainte-Beuve, 6ᵉ
Tel. +33 (0)1 45 48 20 07
From 130€
www.hotelsaintebeuveparis.com

notes

notes

notes

Ines

Nine (for being beautiful and not having a teenage meltdown while helping-out Mom).

Éric Chales, for negotiating the Paris traffic with skill and aplomb.

François, for generously letting us adopt his restaurant, Chartreux, as our HQ for the making of this book.

Zohra, for her extra hours of hard work so the Moms (Sophie and I) could go out and be Parisians.

Violette, who had to do her homework on her own, but still passed with top marks from her teacher.

Denis, for suggesting I might like to turn the computer off after midnight.

Armelle, who reminded us of all the addresses we almost forgot—the brains and nerve center of the operation.

Katia & Valentin, thanks to whom we have no gray hairs, and who are not in the least big-headed.

The cleaners at Teresa Cremisi's office, because we piled it full of clothes for the photo shoot and didn't leave it in the state we found it.

Tuulia, whose office is next to the noisy photocopier where we printed thousands of photos.

Dinky & Aliosha, whose daily walk depended on which neighborhood we were checking out for the book (at least we didn't go past the vets!).

The wonderful bookseller who convinced you to buy this magnum opus … .

The wonderful journalist who sung our praises (the envelope is in the mail …).

Sophie

Pascale Frey and Jean-Marc Savoye for their coaching.

Santiago Boutan and Soledad Bravi who conjured up the fairy designer.

Jeanne Le Bault for his "Parisian" style.

Daphné Bengoa, who always stays focused.

Véronique Philipponnat, Nathalie Dolivo, Erin Doherty, Philomène Piégay, and Anne-Cécile Sarfati, to whom I delivered everything (almost) late because I was running around Paris with la Parisienne. (But Valérie Toranian encouraged me to do it!)

Stéphane and Caroline who got married without me thanks to a certain model who only works on weekends

Cédric, Aramis, and Sienna for their patience, and because they had to let the sheep out without my help.

Suzy … because everyone knows a true Parisienne never dies.

Thanks to APC, Balenciaga, Chanel, Claudie Pierlot, Dior Homme, Éric Bompard, G.H. Bass, La Bagagerie, Notify, Persol, and Roger Vivier for their help styling Nine à la Parisienne (see Part 1).